The Time of the Landscape

To the memory of my mother.
J. R.

The Time of the
Landscape

On the Origins of the Aesthetic
Revolution

Jacques Rancière

Translated by Emiliano Battista

polity

Originally published in French as *Le temps du paysage: Aux origines de la révolution esthétique* © La Fabrique Editions, 2017

This English edition © Polity Press, 2023

This book is supported by the Institut français (Royaume-Uni) as part of the Burgess programme.

INSTITUT
FRANÇAIS
ROYAUME-UNI

Polity Press
65 Bridge Street
Cambridge CB2 1UR, UK

Polity Press
111 River Street
Hoboken, NJ 07030, USA

ISBN-13: 978-1-5095-4814-9 (hardback)
ISBN-13: 978-1-5095-4815-6 (paperback)

A catalogue record for this book is available from the British Library.

Library of Congress Control Number: 2022937839

Typeset in 11 on 14 pt Sabon by
Cheshire Typesetting Ltd, Cuddington, Cheshire
Printed and bound in Great Britain by CPI Group (UK) Ltd, Croydon

The publisher has used its best endeavors to ensure that the URLs for external websites referred to in this book are correct and active at the time of going to press. However, the publisher has no responsibility for the websites and can make no guarantee that a site will remain live or that the content is or will remain appropriate.

Every effort has been made to trace all copyright holders, but if any have been overlooked the publisher will be pleased to include any necessary credits in any subsequent reprint or edition.

For further information on Polity, visit our website: politybooks.com

Contents

Abbreviations

Burke (1757)   Burke, Edmund. *A Philosophical Enquiry into the Origin of Our Ideas of the Sublime and Beautiful*, ed. Adam Phillips. Oxford: Oxford University Press, 1990.

Burke (1790)   Burke, Edmund. *Reflections on the Revolution in France*, ed. Frank M. Turner. New Haven and London: Yale University Press, 2003.

De Luc (1778)   De Luc, Jean-André. *Lettres physiques et morales sur les montagnes et sur l'histoire de la terre et de l'homme*. The Hague: Detune, 1778.

Gilpin (1772)   Gilpin, William. *Observations, Relative Chiefly to Picturesque Beauty, Made in the Year 1772, on Several Parts of England; Particularly the Mountains, and Lakes of Cumberland,*

and Westmoreland, 2 vols. London: R. Blamire, 1792 [1786].

Gilpin (1776)   Gilpin, William. *Observations, Relative Chiefly to Picturesque Beauty, Made in the Year 1776, on Several Parts of Great Britain; Particularly the High-Lands of Scotland*, 2 vols. London: R. Blamire, 1792 [1789].

Hegel (1835)   Hegel, G. W. F. *Aesthetics: Lectures on Fine Art*, 2 vols. Trans. T. M. Knox. Oxford: Clarendon Press, 1988.

Kant (1790)   Kant, Immanuel. *Critique of Judgment*. Trans. James Creed Meredith, revised by Nicholas Walker. Oxford: Oxford University Press, 2007.

Knight (1794)   Knight, Richard Payne. *Landscape: A Didactic Poem*. London: W. Bulmer and Co., 1794.

Price (1794)   Price, Uvedale. *An Essay on the Picturesque, as Compared with the Sublime and the Beautiful; And, on the Use of Studying Pictures, for the Purposes of Improving Real Landscape*. London: J. Robson, 1794.

Price (1810)   Price, Uvedale. *Essays on the Picturesque, as Compared with the Sublime and the Beautiful; And, on the Use of Studying Pictures, for the Purposes of Improving*

Real Landscape, 3 vols. London:
J. Mawman, 1810.

Whately (1770)   Whately, Thomas. *Observations on Modern Gardening, Illustrated by Descriptions*. London: T. Payne, 1770.

Foreword

I should specify the object that gives this book its title. The time of the landscape discussed here is not the time when flowery gardens, majestic mountains, peaceful lakes, or rough and choppy seas started being described in poems or depicted on walls. It is the time when the landscape imposed itself as a specific object of thought. This object of thought was constituted through quarrels about how gardens should be designed, descriptions of parks adorned by classical temples or humble country lanes, narratives of journeys to solitary lakes and mountains, and evocations of mythological or rustic paintings. This book, then, will follow the specific twists and turns of these narratives and quarrels. What they gave rise to is not so much the taste for a spectacle that delights the eyes or elevates the soul, but the experience of a form of unity in sensible diversity capable of changing the configuration of modes of perception and objects of thought that had existed until then. The time of the landscape is the time when the harmony of landscaped gardens, or the disharmony of wild nature, led to an upheaval in the criterion of the beautiful, and even in the meaning of the word "art." That upheaval entailed another, which affected a notion that is as fundamental in common usage as in philosophical reflection: nature. Whatever impacts nature impacts also the society that is supposed to obey its laws. And so the time of the landscape is also the time when the felicitous organization of society borrowed its metaphors from the harmony of fields, forests, and streams.

In Western societies, it is possible to situate this time quite precisely. It coincides with the birth of aesthetics, understood not as a particular discipline but as a regime for how art is seen and thought. It is also contemporary with the French Revolution, understood not as a succession of more or less violent institutional upheavals, but as a revolution in the very idea of what binds a human community together. And it is also the time when the conjunction of these two upheavals brought a common horizon, however hazily, into focus: that of a revolution that is no longer concerned solely with the laws of the state or the norms of art, but with the very forms of sensible experience. This revolution has been at the center of my work for a long time, and is notably at the heart of a book I published in 2011 entitled *Aisthesis: Scenes from the Aesthetic Regime of Art*. That book collects fourteen telling scenes, ranging from the evocation of an ancient statue in ruins in the 1760s to the description of the interiors of the barracks inhabited by poor sharecroppers in the 1930s. I had already indicated there that this list could be expanded, and the present volume can be seen as such an expansion: yet another scene capable of bringing into view the genesis and transformations of a regime of art, and of the common sensible world it outlines. Moreover, "the time of the landscape" fits quite naturally into the network of artistic and political temporalities that I tried to sketch out in *Modern Times*.[1]

I

A Newcomer to the Fine Arts

Painting, as the second kind of formative art, which presents *sensible appearance* in artful combination with ideas, I would divide into that of the beautiful *depiction of nature*, and that of the beautiful *arrangement* of its *products*. The first is *painting proper*, the second *landscape gardening*.[1]

That is how Kant introduced a newcomer to the classification of the fine arts in 1790: the art of "*landscape gardening*," which consists in the "beautiful *arrangement*" of the "*products*" of nature. In so doing, Kant was confirming something that a few seminal works from the period had already recognized. Thomas Whately published his *Observations on Modern Gardening* in London in 1770, and a French translation appeared the following year. In 1779, Christian Cay Lorenz Hirschfeld's five-volume *Theorie der Gartenkunst* appeared simultaneously in German and French.[2] In 1782, Jacques Delille put the new theories into verse in *Les Jardins*, a poem in four cantos that enjoyed considerable success at the time.[3] It was Whately, in fact, who defined the art of landscape gardening as the art of arranging the products of nature in the most perfect manner. And it was also Whately who, in the opening sentence of his Introduction, proclaimed the recent consecration of this art: "Gardening, in the perfection to which it has lately been brought in England, is entitled to a place of considerable rank among the liberal arts."[4]

The question, then, is to know what accounts for this novelty and perfection. The claim would certainly have surprised connoisseurs. Books about the art of landscape gardening had by then been circulating for two centuries already. Some among them had proclaimed its ancient lineage by evoking the orchards of Alcinous (in Book Seven of the *Odyssey*), the mythical hanging gardens of Babylon, and the painted Roman villas described in two often-cited letters by Pliny the Younger. Closer to Whately's time, the Garden of Venus celebrated in *The Dream of Poliphilus*[5] and the Garden of Eden sung by Milton had captured many an imagination, and the culture of Italian literati had inspired the sophisticated architecture of symbolic gardens. Poets and travelers in the seventeenth century had admired the wonders that Salomon de Caus built for the Elector Palatinate in Heidelberg, and that Le Nôtre designed for the French king at Versailles. The arrangement of embroidered parterres (*parterres en broderie*), green rooms (*cabinets de verdure*), bowling-greens, porticos, or labyrinths had been formalized and abundantly illustrated since 1629, when Daniel Loris published *Le Thrésor des parterres* in Geneva. Indeed, the art of gardening seemed already to be celebrating its perfection in 1709, when Dezallier d'Argenville published *La Théorie et la pratique du jardinage*, an encyclopedic work whose full title promises "new designs of parterres, groves, grass-plots, mazes, banqueting rooms, galleries, porticos, terraces, stairs, fountains, cascades," as well as the "manner of making the ground, forming designs suitable to the place, and putting them in execution, according to the principles of geometry," and the "method of setting and raising in little time, all the plants requisite in fine gardens: also the way to find water, to convey it into gardens, and to make basons and fountains for the same. Together with remarks and general rules in all that concerns the art of gardening."[6] We might conclude that the perfection attained there belies the novelty that Whately claimed seventy years later. That conclusion, however, would hide the core of the problem, which turns precisely on knowing what is to be understood by "art" and "perfection." The fact is that, although Dezallier d'Argenville promised innumerable marvels, he was not at all interested in getting the fine arts to welcome into its ranks the art of Le Nôtre and his emulators. On the contrary, it was just at the moment when this science of parterres, bowling-greens, labyrinths, canals, and porticos had fallen into discredit that Whately – and Kant after him – claimed this dignity for it.

This seeming paradox teaches an essential lesson: the dignity of an art is something other than its formal perfection. In general, what we call art is the skill (*savoir-faire*) that a will deploys in order to give matter a form. The ingenuity of the conception and the virtuosity of its execution are one way to recognize the perfection acquired in the exercise of a skill. But that is not the same as knowing what objects they produce, and to what end. Traditionally, the excellence of an art had been defined solely in relation to the latter; indeed, that is how the liberal arts had distinguished themselves from the mechanical arts. The latter produced objects that served the needs of human beings, while the former provided pleasure to those whose spheres of existence extended beyond the simple circle of needs. In order to become a liberal art, the art of gardening had to do more than just increase the amount of science that went into its creations. It had to separate its ends from the two needs – the medicinal and the alimentary – usually associated with the cultivation of plants. It was easy for the art of gardening to distance itself both from the traditional collection of medicinal plants, and from the vegetable garden, whose products were destined for the kitchen. For a long time, though, the art of gardening kept its links to the orchard, where the useful was closely tied to the agreeable. Recent studies have pointed out that the famous gardens of the Villa Lante, in Bagnaia, which served as archetypes for Renaissance gardens in Italy, were sites for the intense cultivation of fruit.[7] John Parkinson, for his part, reminded readers of his *Paradisi in Sole. Paradisus Terrestris*, published in London in 1629, that the plants of the Garden of Eden were not just meant to satisfy hunger, but to please the eyes. On the book's frontispiece, vines, apple trees, pineapples, and date palms are combined with tulips, carnations, cyclamen, and fritillaries to convey the image of an earthly paradise.

The architectural magnificence of Le Nôtre's gardens cut the knot that bound the art of vistas and embroidered parterres to the cultivation of fruit trees. Still, the distance that Le Nôtre established between his art and utility proved to be no more efficient than the perfection of garden designs in gaining for the art of gardening a place among the liberal arts. That is because the excellence that separated the liberal from the mechanical arts could not be measured solely through the pleasure that the talent of the architect provided to members of the very upper classes. In the course of the eighteenth century, the liberal arts had taken on a new name: the fine arts. For an art to gain the title of fine art, it had to do more than provide refined pleasure to the well born. It had to satisfy an autonomous criterion of beauty by producing a specific pleasure rooted in the imitation of nature. "Nature – that is, all of reality plus all that we can readily conceive to be possible – is the prototype or model for the arts."[8] So writes Batteux in *The Fine Arts Reduced to the Same Principle*, a book that was still considered an authority in Kant's time. For Batteux, the word nature does not evoke images of greenery. Rather, to have nature as a model meant two things: to imitate the traits presented by the objects and beings of nature so as to make them recognizable while also rendering them more beautiful; and to imitate – by assembling the visible traits of nature – an invisible nature defined as the perfect combination of its elements into a coherent whole.

For the art of gardening to be elevated to the rank of fine art, it had to do more than simply separate itself from every useful end. It also had to satisfy the criterion through which beautiful works are recognized. In other words, it had to imitate nature – or, rather, "beautiful nature," which is not satisfied with reproducing the traits that render things recognizable, but goes further and assembles the traits, borrowed from the most beautiful models, into a perfect figure that is not to be found in simple nature. This principle is illustrated by the example, so oft-repeated, of Zeuxis, who availed himself of the traits of five different women in order to compose the ideal image of Helen. That is what the "beautiful *arrangement*" of nature's "*products*" had to do: not just transform nature, but imitate it by composing, on the ground itself and using the sparse beauties it dispenses, a superior beauty. A problem emerges, however, when the word nature also starts to mean rolling hills and valleys, green trees and meadows, and trickling streams: how can one imitate nature by using its products? After all, to imitate nature had meant to reproduce its traits in objects that are not natural. Batteux had been quite explicit on this point: unlike the mechanical arts, the fine arts do not *use* nature, they only *imitate* it. The products of the fine arts are not just different from nature, they are its exact opposite: artificial beings. How, then, can the art of gardening – the art that imitates nature with nature's own products – gain entrance without contradiction into the kingdom of the fine arts, given that it breaks one of the fundamental principles of the fine arts?

That is the problem that Kant is trying to find an answer to when he includes the art of landscape gardening in a new division – experimental and provisional, as he himself underlines – of the fine arts. In effect, this inclusion is obliged to take surprising, even paradoxical, paths. The category in which this new art finds its place is that of the figurative (or "formative") arts. This category, according to Kant, can be split in two. Kant ranges on one side the arts of "*sensible truth*," that is to say, the arts that translate ideas into forms we can touch, forms that occupy a material extension in space. These are the plastic arts: architecture and sculpture.

And, on the other side, Kant ranges an art of *"sensible appearance,"* painting, in which the figure does not have spatial reality but paints itself on the eye, as it were, in accordance with its appearance on a plane.[9] At first sight, the art of gardening would seem to belong to the first category, since it clearly corresponds to the criteria of the plastic arts. Its products do have material extension in space: like works of architecture, they are not just seen, but can also be touched. Indeed, it was under the shadow of architectural works that the art of gardening was first individualized, for example with the fantasy gardens by architects like Vignola in sixteenth-century Italy, or with the parks conceived the following century as continuations of the palaces of the Elector Palatinate, the French king, or the Duke of Marlborough. Kant, however, cuts against the grain of this seeming self-evidence. As strange as it may seem, the art of gardening belongs entirely to the division of painting. Certainly no one can deny that it occupies space. But it does so in a way that is quite different from architecture. That is because architecture has two defining traits. The first is that the forms it deploys are arbitrary, that is to say, they depend entirely on the desire of the architect, and not on the imitation of a natural model. The second is that they always pursue a specific end. Whether building a home, a public building, or a commemorative monument, the architect creates something intended to be more than a form to be looked at. There is a defined use for the architect's structure, and that requires a judgment about the adequacy of the thing to its concept. And that criterion pushes the architect's practice toward the side of the mechanical arts. The more perfect the art of the architect is as art, the more the architect is master of the means he borrows from nature in order to achieve his own ends, the less liberal his art is.

If the art of gardening merits inclusion among the liberal arts, it is insofar as it opposes architectural perfection, which depends on the exact realization of an idea by borrowing materials from nature. The beautiful arrangement of the products of nature, conversely, does not treat these products as materials to be used. Like painting, the art of gardening is an art of appearances that imitates appearances. One will object that the art of gardening does not, like painting, produce only the appearance of corporal extension: we walk along its paths, its trees rise up to the sky, we can drift down its streams. But the problem is actually elsewhere. If the art of gardening is an art of appearance, it is because it produces only the appearance of what architecture produces in reality: a spatial construction governed by a specific end. And it is a liberal art because it has no end other than eliciting a specific pleasure: the "play of the imagination in the contemplation of its forms."[10] This allows us to say that Batteux's precept is respected: the art of gardening belongs to the fine arts because what it produces are in fact artificial appearances. According to Kant, it resembles "simple aesthetic painting,"[11] that is, painting that has no defined theme, but instead plays at imitating nature by assembling the elements of air, earth, and water while using nothing more than the resources of light and shadow. Ultimately, nature in landscaped gardens is an imitation of the way painting imitates nature: a play of earth and water, air and light, that is quite well illustrated by Julie's secret garden in *The New Heloise*.

We must be careful not to be duped by the concept of play. It is quite true that the art of gardening lightens the heaviness of the earth and the weight of trees and renders the arrangement of hills and streams more immaterial than the forms produced by sculpture. That does not mean, however, that nature has become a pure play of forms. Rather, it means that the borders between the way nature plays with air, earth, and water, and the way the artist plays with light and shadow on a canvas, have become porous. There is no longer nature as a way of being to be imitated, on one side, and art as a power to create objects that present nature's images, on the other. There is a movement: it starts with the play of natural elements, continues with the play of forms, and enlivens the mental powers so that they are in free play, as are also light and shadow when composing a setting of air, earth, and water. But the latent reference to Rousseau reminds us that this garden-play is just as much a lesson about life as it is about nature. Kant says in the next section (§52): undoubtedly the play of forms is pleasant because it is the execution of a plan. It is like an effect without a cause. But the pleasure it produces is not the indifferent joy of refined minds: it is a "culture" that "disposes the spirit to ideas."[12] If nature in landscaped gardens seems to imitate the landscapes of painters, this disposition to ideas, for its part, finds its models in the beauties of nature. Its vocation, however, is not to represent these beauties. It is to espouse the movement they propose, a movement that releases the imagination from its normal dependence on understanding and in so doing obliges it to go beyond itself toward "ideas." These "ideas" are not what we usually understand by the term: intellectual forms that generate material forms. The world of ideas is rather the still-indeterminate beyond toward which tends the movement through which material forms are made and unmade under the gaze.

That becomes still more evident when free nature becomes "raging" nature and the combinations of air, earth, and water, modulated by light and shadow, assume the aspect of the unformed and the frightening: "Bold, overhanging, and, as it were, threatening rocks, thunderclouds piled up the vault of heaven, borne along with flashes and peals, volcanoes in all their violence of destruction, hurricanes leaving desolation in their track, the boundless ocean rising with rebellious force, the high waterfall of some mighty river (...). The *astonishment* amounting almost to terror, the horror and sacred awe, that seizes us when gazing upon the prospect of mountains ascending to heaven, deep ravines and torrents raging there, deep-shadowed solitudes that invite to brooding melancholy, and the like."[13] We recognize the setting that Kant is sketching with these lines: it is called the sublime. And that, too, is an old story. Kant was writing more than a century after Boileau translated into French verse the *Peri Hypsous*, the treatise where Pseudo-Longinus celebrates the sacred enthusiasm of inspired poets and orators.[14] And more than thirty years after Burke had brought this sacred enthusiasm to the level of poor human beings and made it the humiliating feeling of terror and dread before the majesty of power, the darkness of night, or the menacing vagueness of boundless expansion. Kant set out to put an end to the hegemony of Burke's psychological analysis and to render unto the sublime its dignity as a movement that carries the mind beyond its ordinary regime. The grandeur that cannot be measured – the rocks, thunderclouds, and flashes before which we feel powerless – is not there simply to debase the mind but to lead it toward a higher power of freedom. If the imagination avows its powerlessness, it is the better to show the mind the supersensible kingdom that is its vocation.

We shall revisit the complex relation of solidarity and opposition that links these two thinkers. What interests us for now is neither the particular picture Kant draws, nor the architecture of his book. It is, instead, the displacement of relations between nature and art that make that picture and architecture possible, and which they bear out. In the ancient tradition resurrected by Boileau, the sublime was a particular oratorical and poetical style. Burke made it a feeling of dread before a higher power. With Kant, it took on the form of a *mise-en-scène* in which nature – a certain nature – is the determinant agent: a raging nature that contradicts the peaceful links of cause and effect that had governed art. But also a nature carefully framed in paintings. The images of towering mountains, vertiginous rocks, flashes of thunder and lightning, and raging torrents that Kant invokes are all scenes well ensconced in the imaginary of his time: the Valais mountains that Saint-Preux travels through in *The New Heloise*; the Bernese Highlands described by Jean-André de Luc and painted by Felix Meyer; the red hot lava of Mount Etna described by Patrick Brydone or painted by Joseph Wright of Derby; the mountains and lakes of Cumberland or of the Scottish Highlands that William Gilpin captured both in texts and watercolors; Loutherbourg's stormy skies; the fiery heavens of Joseph Vernet. A raging nature outside itself and yet enclosed by gilded frames, a nature still similar to the paintings that decorated rich households and that could even be found, as stamps, on the desks of scholars.

What introduces itself with the art of gardening into the universe of the fine arts is, apparently, a nature quite different from the one whose principle was to imitate. For Batteux and his brethren, nature illustrated itself in the passions that act on human beings, expressed itself in an inspired line of verse, or was translated into the traits and attitudes of painted or sculpted figures. The new nature, for its part, expresses itself in the play of light and shadow on the slopes and ridges of the landscape. In the past, nature had been identified with the organized connection of causes and effects, and art's function had been to imitate it in its own order. Now, however, nature became a set of effects that, rather than obeying a will working to bring about a specific plan, obliterates the very border between nature and art. Nature ceased to be a model that remains recognizable across the various forms in which it is imitated, and became a movement that runs through and animates the universe of the arts, a movement that comes from elsewhere and goes beyond that universe. We must understand the genesis of this nature in order to see how, with it, the universe of the fine arts recedes in order to make space for this new reality that we call, simply, art.

II
Scenes of Nature

To understand this metamorphosis, we should revisit the specific "perfection" that earned for the art of gardening its new place among the liberal arts. The arguments Whately advances in support of this art's claims to that place merit our attention: "It is as superior to landscape painting, as a reality to a representation: it is an exertion of fancy; a subject for taste; and being released now from the restraints of regularity, and enlarged beyond the purposes of domestic convenience, the most beautiful, the most simple, the most noble scenes of nature are all within its province."[1]

These seemingly banal sentences express a revolution in relation to the norms of the representative regime, and to the "nature" that had served as its foundation. By the standard of those norms, Whately's very first claim is plainly absurd. In the representative regime, the "beautiful nature" that a poet, painter, or sculptor represents is, by definition, superior to nature itself, since the representation assembles traits that are never found combined in a single natural subject. A beautiful painting, one in which the artist has selected and distributed on the planes of a canvas the most picturesque accidents of the ground, the most flattering effects of light, the most appropriate objects, and the most interesting characters will always be superior to even the best tended landscape, subjected as it is to the vagaries of the terrain, the growth of plants, the elements, and the seasons. Moreover, the art of painting, which "takes hold of bodies only," will forever remain subjected to the preeminence of poetry, which alone can "expose to the senses what is insensible," because it alone can show the "inner springs that move the soul and make it visible."[2]

Art's perfection in the representative regime depended on showing these "inner springs." That is how art imitated nature. And, as already mentioned, nature in this instance did not evoke any images of greenery. Indeed, none of the seven definitions of nature in the 1694 edition of the *Dictionnaire de l'Académie* evokes a rustic setting. Nature is "the entirety of the universe"; a "universal spirit present in every created thing and through which these things have their beginning, middle, and end"; and, even, "the inner principle of operation of every being." This inner principle, which connects beings and things in a chain of causes and effects, is not to be found in the charming valleys, streams, or forests that artists can depict, but in how artists connect human behaviors and passions. The Abbé Dubos, a great theoretician of imitation, had already insisted on that point by adhering to the hierarchy of genres of painting: the painter who shows us a basket of flowers or a farmer with his cattle on a country lane produces a mechanical imitation. We admire the skill of the artist who succeeds in reproducing the forms of objects so exactly. But we are not moved by the result, because nature is not on such a canvas. If the landscape deserves to be represented, and if its representation is to be an imitation of nature, then there must be characters who perform actions that move us because they express sentiments and passions whose causal links we recognize.[3]

Whately wrote his treatise fifty years later. He was contemporary with an artist, Thomas Gainsborough, who often painted farmers on country roads, doing things as unremarkable as driving cattle, taking their wares to market, or courting peasant women. Much as the academicians might have turned up their nose at these subjects, it became accepted thenceforward that trees, meadows, and wooded lanes did deserve the name "nature." That does not mean simply that these banal elements of nature, which were not deliberately selected or assembled, merited being painted. It means something more troubling: these elements now claimed to be the "nature" that gave art its norm. The author of the poetry cycle *Les Saisons* (The Seasons) gives this identification its most succinct expression: "the ancients loved and sang the countryside; we admire and sing nature."[4] What expresses itself in the charms of the countryside is nature as a singular power. That is why the art of gardening can claim to be superior to the art of landscape painting: the spectacles it composes directly capture the beautiful, simple, or noble scenes that nature unfolds without the help of art – or, rather, that nature unfolds as an artist.

That is what is radically new: this nature that now makes itself known through the assembly of trees, bodies of water, and stones across an expanse of land is more than just a model to be imitated by artists. It is itself an artist. Its art consists of presenting scenes. The word *scene* – which features prominently in Whately's pages, as well as in the pages of the British authors who described gardens and landscapes in his wake – would have been surprising to a French audience, which is why his translator felt compelled to add a somewhat embarrassed footnote about it. In it, he begs readers to be indulgent about "certain expressions borrowed from the language of morals and the theater, like scene and character,"[5] which would have been difficult for the translator to replace. These expressions are indeed loaded with meaning. They say that nature is a theatrical artist. And drama, because of its capacity to give visible expression to an invisible nature, was the highest form of the poetry that served as the model for the figurative, or "formative," arts. Dubos argued that artists made up for the poverty of lanes and woods by turning them into sets for the living drama of human passions. Whately replied that the set – the ground, woods, stones, and bodies of water – is itself a scene: it presents a visible spectacle, one that "exposes to the senses what is insensible" by enlivening, above and beyond the pleasures of the eye, the intellectual powers of taste and imagination. Whately does add a condition, though: the art of gardening has this power because it has been "released now from the restraints of regularity."[6]

This argument, too, is not devoid of paradox. If there was a virtue that the representative logic recognized as common to art and nature, it was precisely that regularity. The word nature meant obedience to necessary laws, while the word art meant the invention of fables or figures whose arrangement imitated that necessity. It was well understood that art should not make its regularity overly stiff. To imitate nature actually meant two things: to produce a work whose laws of composition are as rigorous as those by which nature binds beings to its necessity; but, also, to imitate the way nature's appearance dissimulates the rigor of that bond. The art of imitation had to have the same allure of freedom and "ease" of nature, which manifests neither will nor labor in how it produces its effects. That art had to imitate nature as a (necessary) cause and as a (free) effect.

This balance is broken when nature itself becomes an artist, and when its art manifests itself as the creation of scenes that combine trees, water streams, and stones with the play of light and shadow. Thenceforward, nature meant, essentially, freedom. That freedom is what is celebrated in the lines by Saint-Lambert that Whately's translator added as an epigraph to the book: "Behold, in these fields and woods, emancipated nature / Freely giving itself over to its noble energy." Humboldt, a man of science who understood very well that the invisible work of terrestrial layers is the cause of the luxurious vegetation offered to sight, agreed: "Nature is the domain of freedom."[7] Freedom is not licentiousness, as any schoolchild whose curriculum includes the classics knows. It is not a pure anarchic dispersion. If nature merits its name, it is because its principle is singular. And if nature is an artist, it is because its "free energy" likewise obeys the same principle that governs the productions of the arts of imitation: unity in variety. The whole question, then, turns on how to think a specific mode of unity, one that rebels against the regularity accomplished in the scene.

One way to think that mode is based on the simple opposition between two types of lines and surfaces.

Regularity has two essential characteristics: symmetry and right angles. And these two characteristics are combined in what became quite early on the anti-nature model: the geometric garden, in which rectilinear and unshaded lanes, imposing statues, and trees mutilated by the topiary art serve as mirrors to the pride of their master. Such is Timon's Villa, whose exact symmetry is for Alexander Pope the image of an inverted nature:

> Grove nods at grove, each alley has a brother,
> And half the platform just reflects the other.
> The suff'ring eye inverted Nature sees,
> Trees cut to statues, statues thick as trees.[8]

Authors throughout the century would go on to cite or paraphrase these lines, as well as Shaftesbury's denunciation of the "formal Mockery of Princely gardens,"[9] and Addison's opposition of the "rough careless strokes of nature" to the "nice touches and embellishments of art."[10] But we must be careful not to misunderstand: the nature that these authors held up as a model is still not, for all that, praised as an artist creating scenes. Nor does it evoke the deep solitudes or the unbridled elements that would go on to charm the authors of the generation that followed. It is, simply, the "nature of things," their authentic order, which they pit against human pretensions in two of its forms: that of the prince or lord who wants to upset that order so as to inscribe on the ground the image of his grandeur; and that of the man of art who puts his geometric science and creative pride at the service of that ambition.

What they pit against the anti-nature of France, marked by Cartesian geometrism and monarchic absolutism, is an English model of natural unity. This model was constructed around three characteristics, though it was not long before they found themselves in tension and started to define opposing "natures." The opposition to the stiffness of the geometric garden was first articulated through the *vastness* that Addison invokes in the articles he published between 1710 and 1712, in the *Tatler* and then in the *Spectator*. Vastness is not necessarily an infinite expanse, but an expanse that opens to the imagination the possibility of prolonging what it sees by ignoring the division that characterizes both the symmetrical parterres of the art of gardening and the barriers that property imposes on the landscape. Then it was the *intricacy* that William Hogarth, in *The Analysis of Beauty*, defines as the variation of the line that leads the eye – and the mind with it – in a "chace" by not allowing it ever to fix on one spot.[11] And, lastly, it was a particular form of *intricacy*, one that tends to free itself from the first in order to assert itself as the absolute criterion of the beautiful: the serpentine line that Hogarth was the first to define, but which went on to become a cornerstone of Burke's theory of the beautiful. For Burke, the curved, waving line whose direction changes continually and imperceptibly is the characteristic that nature and art have in common. That line is both the natural beauty of bodies, exemplified by the female neck and breasts – "the smoothness; the softness; the easy and insensible swell; the variety of the surface, which is never for the smallest space the same"[12] – and the perfection of the sculptural art. On the one hand, the model of the female body brings wild nature, which could evoke the criteria of vastness and intricacy, into the smooth forms of artistic beauty. But, on the other hand, it is strictly opposed to another body, which governs another art:

the architectural body inherited from Vitruvius. There was no shortage of ancient temples in the model gardens of eighteenth-century England. But the place of their rectilinear colonnades was carefully determined by the undulations of the ground, with its "smooth" and "soft" inclines and its easy and insensible "swells."

A first alliance of these three criteria was thus established under the hegemony of one of them: the waving or serpentine line. That is how the model of the free English garden was formed, with vast vistas punctuated by well-isolated clumps of trees, softly undulating lawns, sinewy alleys, and bodies of water whose smoothed banks were skirted by serpentine paths. This model is illustrated by the exemplary gardens of the time: Stowe's Garden, created by the still quite rectilinear art of the royal architect Charles Bridgeman, but brought into harmony with the new ideas by the recognized father of the art of the English garden, William Kent, and even more so by his successor, Lancelot Brown; Painshill Park, designed for his own use by Charles Hamilton, who squandered his fortune importing trees from America; or Leasowes Gardens, fashioned after the fantasies of the poet William Shenstone. Lancelot Brown, the uncontested master of this art, was nicknamed Capability Brown, because he claimed to be able to judge the "capability for improvement" of the gardens that he was invited to transform and bring into alignment with the new ideas.

Burke, speaking about the serpentine line, says that the eye is seized by vertigo as it tries in vain to find an endpoint. But it is the eye and mind of readers today that are seized by vertigo as they try to follow the minute, step-by-step descriptions of the promenades that reveal the charms of these gardens. As an introduction to

Shenstone's poems, Robert Dodsley, the volume's editor and publisher, provided an exhaustive description of Leasowes Gardens. Throughout Dodsley's twenty-seven pages, the reader/visitor is invited to ascend and descend in lockstep with the casual allure of the winding paths that skirt the curves, themselves winding, of lakes with softened banks, or of streams that lead to winding valleys or flow along the foot of circular and softly sloping hills, which can be climbed without effort by means of lanes that snake their way through tree groves with winding lines until the reader/visitor arrives upon benches from where the eye can see far into the distance and take in yet more streams winding their way through still more winding valleys.

The serpentine line would thus seem to condense in itself all the virtues of *intricacy*. As it happens, though, the narrative of these endless windings is interrupted to make space for descriptions of elements of the landscape that are not so softly rounded. That is the case, in Leasowes, with the "irregular and romantic fall of water" that runs "one hundred and fifty yards in continuity." The water volume may be limited, but the "intricacy of the scene," coupled with "the concealed height from whence it [the water] flows," results in spectators "without reflection, add[ing] the idea of magnificence to that of beauty."[13] We realize at this point that the intricacy of these gardens cannot be reduced to the insensible variations of the curved line. The rocks must invest the scene with ruggedness, and the irregularity of the separation of waters must create a variety that accentuates the play of light. The very things that conceal the visible spectacle must expand it, and the beauty of the soft rustling of the waters must be transformed into magnificence through an imagination that flits toward their invisible source. In contrast to the limit, the smoothness, and the delicacy that define beauty for Burke, the intricacy that allows a landscaped setting to be called a scene of nature reveals itself to be asperity and rupture, indistinction and boundlessness. This points to the fact that the alliance between intricacy and the curved line conceals a latent tension between two opposing principles. This tension is still concealed in Dodsley's description of the poet's garden. In the 1790s, however, it would become an explicit contradiction in the offensive led against improvers who, following Brown, had started fashioning vast spaces that give onto soft undulations and sinewy paths.[14] This critique is summed up by two men. Both were landowners who were proud of their gardens. But they were also men of letters, art lovers formed by the Grand Tour and the discovery of Italy and its painting collections, and progressive minds. Not revolutionary minds, certainly, but minds sensitive to the events in France. One is Richard Payne Knight, the other Uvedale Price.

What they reproach in Brown's style is the same thing that Pope and Burke had reproached in Dutch or French gardens: their uniformity. It is not enough, however, to pit the curved line against the straight line and soft undulations against geometric terraces. Deep down, they all share the same principle, which is that of an art that imposes its artificial order on nature in order to display its own skill and please the vanity of landowners. To achieve their soft undulations, new landscapists have to flatten out the ground and cut away anything that juts out. To open up wide vistas, they must cut into the densely packed trees in order to isolate two or three large ones and thus produce the *clumps* that, "placed like beacons on the summits of hills,"[15] solemnly punctuate the landscape. And they must encircle their park with *belts* of trees that separate it from the surrounding countryside. In short, in the name of the curved line they follow the same approach as the architects of the rectilinear gardens in France. They, too, are *levelers*, fanatics of the even. If the geometric order of parterres, compartments, and bowling-greens reflected the vanity of princes, the large open spaces, sinewy paths, clumps, and belts of the new style translated, at least to their critics, the pride of landowners who treat the landscape as their possession and impose these twists and turns on their unfortunate visitors so as to make them experience expanse through serpentine paths. In his didactic poem, *The Landscape*, Richard Payne Knight describes the torments of the unfortunate visitor, who is thus led from "vale" to hill and back again, only to end with an ironic piece of advice:

> But why not rather, at the porter's gate
> Hang up the map of all my lord's state
> Than give his hungry visitor the pain
> To wander o'er so many miles in vain?[16]

The art of the serpentine line and of soft volumes is essentially an art for ornamenting properties – indeed, it is little more than a simple cartography of the property. In order to become a liberal art, understood as an art free from utilitarian servitude, the art of gardening has to change methods. It has to learn from the scenes that nature itself composes. As it happens, there is a specific quality to that form of composition. That quality, which eludes the division that Burke establishes between the

23

politeness of beauty and the terror of the sublime, came to be called the picturesque. Strictly speaking, the adjective means simply that which provides a good subject for a painting. But this minimal definition actually hides a revolution in the relation between nature and art. In the classical definition, nature – in the empirical sense, as the set of things available to the senses – does nothing more than supply the materials that the art of imitation selects and perfects in order to produce a work that corresponds to ideal nature, which consisted of an invisible link between causes and effects. Now, however, this nature available to the senses, this nature without interiority and composed of expanses of earth and water, gives art not just its materials, but also its models of composition – models that art is not certain to be able to match, and that in any case entail a new idea of nature, of art, and of the relation between them.

Nature is an artist of a very peculiar sort, one superior to every other artist because it is not trying to make art. That is why its scenes provide the perfect models for the forms and compositions that art must appropriate. Like every artist, and better than every artist, nature composes its scenes by linking two essential operations: the division into parts, and the assembly of those parts into a whole. The specificity of picturesque beauty is anchored to these two points: the nature of the parts, and the model of their assembly. And it is on these two points that the two great theoreticians of the picturesque, William Gilpin and Uvedale Price, disagree. In 1782, Gilpin published *Observations on the River Wye and Several Parts of South Wales etc., Relative Chiefly to Picturesque Beauty, Made in the Summer of the Year 1770*. That work was followed, in 1786, by similar

Observations, made in the year 1772, of the mountains and lakes of Cumberland and Westmorland, and in 1789 by *Observations* of the Scottish Highlands made in 1776. Price, for his part, published in 1794 a work entitled *An Essay on the Picturesque, as Compared with the Sublime and the Beautiful; And, on the Use of Studying Pictures, for the Purpose of Improving Real Landscape.* We could say, summarizing things, that Gilpin focuses his analyses on the mode of division into parts that creates the picturesque, while Price insists on how a multiplicity of elements merges into a holistic effect.

Gilpin's whole analysis is anchored to a reasoning that nearly borders on the self-evident: for there to be a composition, there must be parts. And for there to be parts, there must be breaks and fragmentation. Gilpin is quite removed from the smoothness dear to Burke: according to him, the ruggedness of the objects and the breaks in the lines are what give the landscape its structure and make it interesting to the eyes and the imagination. Anyone who has ventured beyond landscaped parks and roamed the wild and mountainous regions of Cumberland, Scotland, or Wales will quickly notice, *a contrario*, this virtue of fragmentation: the *formal* character of a circular lake with perfectly smoothed banks is boring, and the *massive* character of softly rounded mountains is unpleasant. What gives mountains their picturesque aspect are lines that break gradually into layers. The fractured rocks and the broken ground animate the landscape and give rise to the different mosses, gravels, and vegetation that tint it with so much variety. The different cavities and fractures capture the light and showcase its play with shadow. They also account for the superior charm of waterfalls where uneven rocks divide the water and create pockets of vegetation over those that fall in a single straight line. Promontories and recesses animate the banks of lakes, and the islets that dot their surface give them variety. There would be no point in pitting the serene beauty of immobile lakes against this analysis, because that beauty depends on the contrast with the accidental reliefs of the surrounding mountains. What the eye perceives as it approaches the immobile lake is not the reality of a peaceful volume of water, but the appearance of an expanse broken by a variety of shadows, by the undulations of the surface, and by the reflection of the more or less "rugged" objects that surround it. And these breaks are evidently magnified by those produced by the alternations of sun and shadow or passing clouds, not to mention the tempests that sometimes stir up the waters into waves, or the flashes of lightning that cut across the sky and are reflected on the lake's surface.

The ruptures thus form the very structure of the landscape. That is why rounded lines and desolate expanses can themselves become elements of a picturesque composition when they contrast with slopes animated by scree or by the variety of colors of the vegetation. The opposition of the unified and the broken runs through the elements that form a landscape and defines a specific mode of vision, a picturesque way of linking the whole to the parts. This rejects the dominant and global vision of the panorama. That is why Gilpin deplores the indiscreet zeal of the guide who takes him to the panoramic perspective of Derwentwater, a cherished site in Cumberland: "But he, who is in quest of the picturesque scenes of the lake, must travel along the rough side-screens that adorn it; and catch its beauties, as they arise in smaller portions – its little bays, and winding shores – its deep recesses, and hanging promontories – its garnished rocks, and distant mountains."[17]

The relation of the unified and the fractured defines both the uncompassed work of nature-as-artist, and the way nature divides into scenes offered to the compass of the artist's eye. That is what Gilpin describes in the Watendlath Valley: "Not only the design, and composition, but the very stroke of nature's pencil might be traced through the whole scene; every fractured rock, and every hanging shrub, which adorned it, was brought within the compass of the eye: each touch so careless, and yet so determined: so wildly irregular; and yet all conducing to one whole."[18]

That is how the art of a freed nature, a nature that is an artist because it does not try to make art, manifests itself. The rudeness of its elements and the irregularities of their disposition offer, to those who know how to look, the principles for the just unity in variety of the whole: the unity that is founded on contrast. It is with the compass of this gaze on the uncompassed work of nature that Gilpin travels through mountains and valleys, or follows the streams and lakes of wild regions. That is why, however removed the mountains and valleys where he hunts for the picturesque may be, the latter is defined always through a certain architectural grammar of forms. It is on that point that Uvedale Price's analysis differs. For him, there is no picturesque *line*. That is the lesson taught by these ruins that painters love to reproduce and that landscapists try to imitate with their creations. The charm of the famous Temple of the Sybil in Tivoli does not come from its round and smooth form – that is, from the qualities that define beauty for Burke. Richard Payne Knight will see, even in the rugged and compact stone, the exemplary refutation of the philosopher's theory of beauty.[19] Price, for his part, remains faithful to that theory. Which does not mean that he does not share Knight's ideas: the effect produced by the temple does not have to do with the line. The determining element, rather than being the form, is in fact an accident. This accident is not just the work of time, which has worn and partially ruined the stone. It is the very nature of this local stone: rough and dingy, and undoubtedly used by the architect for simple economic reasons, it presents in its current state a beauty of tint and surface that the work of time would have effaced on a finer marble.[20]

The lesson is exemplary: the beauty of an illustrious ruin, copied hundreds of times by landscape painters, can be attributed to the same two causes that explain the superiority of "unimproved" parks and forests over those "improved" by Brown: "accident and neglect."[21] Accident is not the same as chance. It is not, as some recommended, a question of randomly distributing the vegetation, as if the seeds had been sown by a bird. Accident is the specific work of that which was not chosen or willed. Nature is an artist giving lessons to the arts, but not because it offers exemplary lines or surfaces, but because it refuses the principle that served as the norm to every art worthy of its name: selection. Nature's defining trait is that it does not select or distinguish. Instead, it allows the coexistence of all manner of objects, all varieties of forms, colors, light, and shadow.

The absence of selection accomplishes the principle of unity in variety by combining natural elements through the randomness of their development, be that the random work of time and the seasons, or of the activities that have impacted them. That is how it produces the unifying effect that the art of gardening must imitate: not through the collection of selected parts, but through the fusion of an infinity of constant elements and accidental circumstances. What must be imitated in nature is its blind way of working, which sometimes appropriates the results of human activity. Price recommends that the creator of artificial lakes should observe how nature itself creates lakes in miniature and vegetation that reflects itself on them by using the holes and heaps of earth that workers leave behind them in abandoned gravel pits.[22] And against the stiffness of clumps and belts that isolate and magnify the property, Price pits, not a virginal and primitive nature, but a familiar nature marked by the traces of ordinary human activity and by the carelessness of art: that of "hollow lanes" and "bye roads," where

> ... a thousand circumstances of detail, promote the natural intricacy of the ground; the turns are sudden and unprepared; the banks sometimes broken and abrupt; sometimes smooth, and gently but not uniformly sloping; now wildly over-hung with thickets of trees and bushes, now loosely skirted with wood; no regular verge of grass, no cut edges, no difficult lines of separation; all is mixed and blended together and the border of the road itself, shaped by the mere tread of passengers and animals, is as unconstrained as the footsteps that formed it: even the tracks of the wheels (for no circumstance is indifferent) contribute to

the picturesque effect of the whole; the lines they describe are full of variety; they just mark the way among trees and bushes, while any obstacle, a cluster of low thorns, a furze-bush, a tussock, a large stone, will force the wheels into sudden and intricate turns, at the same time those obstacles themselves, either wholly or partially concealing the former ones, add to that variety and intricacy.[23]

Through the neglect that allows the vegetation to grow on its own, and through the accident that imprints upon it the seal of circumstances, the elements of nature are linked under our gaze in a way that is entirely para-doxical from the point of view of art, under our gaze. Indeed, it is because everything is fused that every-thing is *connected*. This point is borne out in another instance: on the same hollow lanes, the pollards of mutilated old tree trunks stretch their branches every which way, sometimes even across the lanes themselves. That which partially covers the view contributes to the *intricacy* that gives the scene its character. And what *obstructs* the path is likewise what makes it a path of communication. The tree whose branches jut out in all directions had been a major figure in the gardening imaginary of the English ever since Addison opposed its disordered luxuriance to the geometrically cut shrubs and artificial forms of the topiary art. But this tree had somehow gained aristocratic credentials by isolating itself in the majestic solitude of the "clumps." It even managed to become, under Burke's quill, a metaphor for the aristocracy as an essential component of the social landscape. The enemies of clumps, however, were never shy about observing that the same lords who want clumps to tower over their free lawns also planted, in close rows and behind the enclosures that now isolated and protected their properties, pines and poplars from Italy. The tree whose branches stretch across lanes thus becomes a metaphor for a natural order undisturbed by the artificial divisions of art and property: not the imagined nature of noble savages, but simply a familiar and shared universe in which the same undergrowth and branches that obstruct the lane make it a path open to everyone. This universe is *one*, though not because of the arrangement of its parts but, on the contrary, because it is not composed of parts, because it is devoid of dividing lines, and is, in a way, even devoid of lines altogether. Richard Payne Knight, the most radical reformer of the art of gardening, puts it this way: "For nature, still irregular and free / Acts not by lines, but general sympathy."[24]

Knight published those lines in 1794. At the end of the following year – year IV of the French Republic – Denis Diderot's *Essais sur la peinture* (Essays on Painting), which had till then remained in manuscript form, were posthumously published in Paris. A theme that runs through its seven chapters is the unity that spreads autonomously over the surface of a body or canvas: the harmony of movements (*conspiration des mou-vements*), the general hue that the sky spreads over objects, the infinite reflection of shadows and bodies that generate harmony, the general light – of nature, of the artists who observe it carefully, and of enlightened nations.[25] Sympathy, understood as the unity born from mixture itself, was the master word of the final years of the eighteenth century. It is a unity felt all the more strongly because it is unseen. This sympathy is likewise what the gaze of the sensible man perceives among the wild mountains of Cumberland, or along the familiar country lanes of Herefordshire. It is the character that makes a scene worthy of being painted because it is the trait shared in common by a free nature and by an art whose school is this artist without a master.

III

The Landscape as
Painting

Every person of the least observation, must have remarked how *broad* the lights and shadows are on a fine evening in nature, or (what is almost the same thing) in a picture of Claude.[1]

With these lines, Uvedale Price comments on a notion that he sees as essential to the pictorial art: breadth. What is immediately striking about this passage, however, is the near-equivalence it posits between a fine evening in nature and a painted canvas. We must be sure to understand him right: Price is not saying that a picture by Claude Lorrain is beautiful because, when we see it, we believe ourselves to be in nature, like the birds who thought the grapes painted by Zeuxis were real. He is saying something else: anyone who wants to understand the principles of the pictorial art must observe how nature itself paints in a way that has nothing to do with art. But if that same person wants to understand the type of unity that gives beauty to a fine evening in nature, he should look at the rectangle of canvas, which the painter has bathed in an evening light that envelops the silhouettes of every object and figure in the same warm tonality. That is why the art of gardening can be considered, without paradox, a division of painting. It is not a matter of saying that the art of gardening must strive to reproduce the landscapes of painters. It is understood that the art of beautifully arranging the products of nature must draw its inspiration from the way that nature itself unconsciously produces such arrangements. But one must learn to see those arrangements, to discern the forms in which air, earth, water, and vegetation have fused in order to produce, along with light and shadow, a singular scene.

Things might seem simple. After all, had not Price himself already showed us how to see such arrangements in the banality of a hollow lane, and even in the miniature lakes formed in the holes of abandoned gravel pits? Still, it is crucial, first, to have developed the habit of pausing to contemplate such insignificant spectacles; second, to have the idea that what one sees in them is, strictly speaking, nature at work; and, third, to conclude that what must be imitated is precisely that work. None of these is self-evident, and all of them require an education. But a new kind of education. Regardless of how well read they may have been, the Abbé Dubos and his peers could not see nature in the image of a farmer driving his cattle on a country road – unless, perhaps, there were a few lines from Virgil to give the image some nobility. Incidentally, that is why such lines were engraved in abundance on the temples, grottos, and benches of such gardens as Stourhead, Stowe, and Leasowes. But no poet could help these men of letters see in puddles of water, twisted trees, clumps of furze, or the ruts that carts hollow out on the road anything other than obstructions to circulation.

No poet, certainly. But painters, maybe. First among these would have been the painters, from the time of Claude Lorrain and Poussin, who developed the habit of settling in Rome, a tradition continued by Richard Wilson and a few others. For many years already, young men of letters from the kingdom, like Uvedale Price and Richard Payne Knight, had met them during the Grand Tour, and returned to their manors with paintings or sketches of the Roman countryside, some with mythological themes, and some without. Then there were the painters who never left England, but who went to those very manors to paint their owners. Some of these painters, if they had something of the plebeian in their soul, would sometimes also paint the trees, lanes, mills, and cottages of the estates. That was the case with Thomas Gainsborough, who was more sensitive than anyone to the charm of rustic lanes and ponds, but who was obliged to earn his living by painting portraits of their owners. At Foxley, the Prices' family estate, he painted the portrait of Uvedale's parents. But he also painted the oaks that lined the roads, and that the tenant-farmers (*métayers*) had the unfortunate habit of polling; if tradition is to be believed, he even took Uvedale, a young boy at the time, as his guide during walks in the woods. And, of course, it is a painting by Gainsborough – or, at any rate, a painting that could easily have been his – that Price describes with his hollow lane invaded by vegetation and rutted by the wheels of a cart similar to the cart on its way to market that Gainsborough depicts in a famous painting. Nor does Price try to hide this: his expressed design, announced in the very title of his book, is to urge landscape architects to use the work of painters as their models. Underneath the title, Price cites the following lines from Cicero as an epigram: "*Quam multa vident pictores in umbris et eminentia quae nos non videmus.*"[2] And he spells out the consequence already in the opening chapter:

> and with respect to the art of improving [gardens], we may look upon pictures as a set of experiments of the different ways in which trees, buildings, water, &c. may be disposed, grouped, and accompanied, in the most beautiful and striking manner, and in every style, from the most simple and rural, to the grandest and most ornamental. Many of those objects, that are scarcely marked as they lie scattered over the face of nature, when brought together in the compass of a small space of canvas are forcibly impressed upon the eye, which by that means learns how to separate, to select, and combine.[3]

Separate, select, and combine: these terms belong to the traditional lexicon of *mimesis*. But those who had used them until then had never thought to associate those operations to unwieldy tree branches, irregular water streams, or ruined architectural forms – and even less to the roots and ruts of a country road. The real issue here is the dignity of the subjects, but, much more importantly, the fact that the process of selection was seen as operating within a nature conceived as a repertory of forms. Price, for his part, uses the same terms to describe something closer to a scenography of incidents. What must be observed are natural forms that attest to the process of their formation or, inversely, unformed spectacles that bear in themselves the virtuality of definite forms. Such were the stains or breaks on old walls

Frontispiece of John Parkinson's *Paradisi in sole. Paradisus Terrestris* (London, 1629)

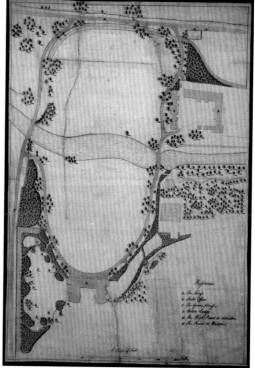

Lancelot Brown, plan for Audley End Park, Essex, England. Photo © Historic England Archive (PLB_N890002)

Claude Lorrain, *Landscape with Aeneas at Delos* (1672).
Photo © Artefact/Alamy Stock Photo

Stourhead Park, Wiltshire, England. Photo © Wirestock,
Inc./Alamy Stock Photo

Harewood, a park by Lancelot Brown, painted
by J. M. W. Turner

Downton, property of Richard Payne Knight

Leasowes Gardens, designed by the poet Richard Shenstone, 1811.
Photo © Chronicle/Alamy Stock Photo

Derwentwater, in Cumberland, England. Arthur Hughes.
Royal Albert Memorial Museum, Exeter, Devon, UK
© Royal Albert Museum/Bridgeman Images

Ullswater Lake, engraving from a William Gilpin watercolor

View of lake from a boat, engraving from a William Gilpin
watercolor

Rocky landscape, engraving from a William Gilpin watercolor

Thomas Gainsborough, *Study of Beech Trees at Foxley* (1760);
Foxley was the Price family estate. Photo © akg-images

Thomas Gainsborough, *The Cottage Door* (c. 1785).
Photo © Artefact/Alamy Stock Photo

Johan Christian Dahl, *Eruption of the Volcano Vesuvius* (1823).
Photo © Heritage Image Partnership Ltd/Alamy Stock Photo

Felix Meyer, *The Lower Grindelwald Glacier* (1700)

Improvements, two satirical engravings

that Leonardo urged us to observe.[4] Such also were the stones, roots, and mosses that Gainsborough took to his studio and used as models for his foregrounds: not just handy accessories, but witnesses to the productive nature of forms.

The great lesson that landscape artists can learn from painters does not have to do with the creative process. It goes without saying that painters have trade secrets that cannot be appropriated by everyone. Nor can one demand the creators of gardens to have the technical ability of the masters of the pictorial art. But one can demand that they learn to look at the world like those masters. Painting is first and foremost an art or science of the gaze. That is why Price feels compelled to spell out what he means by the word: "When I speak of a painter, I do not mean merely a professor, but any man (artist or not) of a liberal mind, with a strong feeling of nature as well as art, who has been in the habit of comparing both together."[5] To be a painter is first and foremost a question of looking. Of a liberal gaze. As it happens, the notion of "liberality" was itself in the process of undergoing a change of meaning. It used to mean a type of activity or pleasure available only to so-called "free" men, that is to say, men not subjected to the constraints of daily needs. Now, conversely, it started being applied to this type of gaze, which no longer associates the quality of a spectacle to a social dignity, but instead separates, as Kant does, the aesthetic appreciation of a building's form from the appreciation of the way of life of its inhabitants. That, according to Price and Knight, is the lesson in "liberalism" that painters can give to improvers, who compose gardens that render sensible the expanse of an estate and the majesty of its owner.

What they can learn from painters is this curious gaze, which finds happy compositions in the most confused and meager spectacles offered by the rural life that surrounds those same estates. It might be nothing more than the confusion of a country lane encumbered by vegetation. But it could also be the extreme mundaneness of a canvas that Philips Wouwerman painted specifically to disgust the upper classes: "the principal objects were a dung-cart just loaded; some carrion lying on the dung; a dirty fellow with a dirty towel; the dunghill itself, and a dog, that from his attitude, seemed likely to add to it."[6] What the art of painting shares with nature is this virtue of connection, which ignores both the dignities of society and the boundaries of property. That is what Wouwerman's peasant scenes share with Lorrain's heroic landscapes, where "temples and palaces, are often so mixed with trees, that the tops overhang their balustrades, and the luxuriant branches shoot between the openings of their magnificent columns and porticos."[7] The creators of picturesque gardens must draw inspiration from this virtue of connection.

It was by pressing on that point that improvers, stung by how Price and Knight mocked them, thought they could get their revenge. They note that their censors actually have no professional experience at all in gardening. Beyond the transformations they had undertaken on their own estates, all they knew about gardens came from the rustic landscapes painted by Hobbema, Ruysdael, or Berchem, the noble landscapes by Titian, Poussin, or Claude Lorrain, and the wild landscapes of Salvator Rosa. They claim that the art of gardening is essentially a matter of being able to judge the felicitous effects produced by the mixture of forms and colors, shadow and light. They pit this *liberal* knowledge, which composes unity from the paradoxical virtues of accident and neglect, to the tasteless mundaneness that judges the appositeness of buildings and gardens to their ends, and the suitability of this or that ornament to this or that place. But, their critics counter, composing a canvas and designing a living space and its environs are two very different things. Knight urges landscapists to draw their inspiration from artists who show "men," not as they are, *"but as they seem'd to be."*[8] How is such a principle applicable to the art of gardening, which does not create shadows but real things? The painter can pick and choose a subject that allows him to lay out the characters, buildings, and flora in a way that respects the canonical tri-partition of planes: the foreground, where the action is situated; the middle ground, which provides relief; and the background, which fades gradually into a blueish atmosphere. In search of these three planes, or "divisions," the artist "rambles over the face of nature until he finds them; or supplies them from the storehouse of his own imagination. But the rural artist is fixed to a given spot [...]. The foreground is much within the power of his art, the middle ground he may generally assist, but the further distances, if he can catch any, are mostly beyond the reach of his control."[9] Those who criticize clumps in the name of Claude's "intricate" branches and leaves forget that trees do not grow on the countryside as quickly as they do on canvases, and that nature needed centuries to give the landscapes that they hold up as examples their present form. They reject the *adequacy* and *propriety* of buildings and ornaments in the name of the "connection" of the whole. But the connection they talk about is for the gaze only. In sum, the buildings and gardens they talk about are to be seen, not inhabited. One need look no further for proof of this than at Price praising those paintings by Claude where tree branches shoot between the openings of columns and porticos. "From this it seems that the Essayist proposes to view from without, and to throw the house into the general composition. And who would not wish to view a house, thus over-grown with trees, rather than go into it, to partake of the damps and unwholesomeness which it must necessarily contain?"[10] The house that is "connected" to the landscape is one that cannot be lived in. The conclusion to be drawn, clearly, is that the two arts must be separated, since landscape painting "has no alliance whatever to Rural ornament: the manual operations of the one have not the least affinity to those of the other."[11]

These criticisms are certainly grounded in good sense. Still, the authors who stress the difference between the appearance that offers itself to the gaze and the reality of the estate and the home misrecognize the weight of what they are saying. It is true that Price and Knight have no professional gardening experience. But what they want to do is pit a broad humanist view against the narrow vision of gardening professionals. And what they propose is not an effective method for designing parks, but a way to reform the gaze. This reform is of course not practicable in the art of gardening, where their principle, incidentally, is to intervene as little as possible. But it does find its place in the upheaval in the criteria of art, the beautiful, and their relation to life that marks the passage from one regime of art to another. What Humphry Repton, William Marshall, and a handful of others say in mocking tones is, after all, identical to what professor Immanuel Kant had already said in very serious tones in a work published five years earlier: the art of gardening is "for the eye only, just like painting."[12] It belongs to the art of sensible appearance, in which the figure has no spatial reality but simply paints itself on the eye in accordance with its appearance on a plane. In that respect, the art of gardening is at once more liberal and closer to nature than the arts of sensible truth, which translate their ideas into solid volumes in space. Kant's classification reflects the mutation that displaced the art of gardening, pushing it away from the solid realities of architecture and toward the appearances of painting. Whately had already underlined that mutation when he defined the place of buildings in gardens. The *expressive* character of the buildings had to be determined, not by their function, but by the scene to which they belonged: "As objects they are designed either to *distinguish*, or to *break*, or to *adorn*, the scenes to which they are applied."[13] On the one hand, they break the monotony of a uniform expanse by introducing variety into lawns, woods, and streams, all of which ran the risk of being far too similar. On the other hand, they enhance the character of the scene. Whately writes:

> Nor do they [buildings] stop at fixing an uncertainty, or removing a doubt; they raise and enforce a character already marked: a temple adds dignity to the noblest, a cottage simplicity to the most rural scenes; the lightness of a spire, the airiness of an open rotunda, the splendor of a continued colonade, are less ornamental than expressive.[14]

That is why one must neither include more buildings than is strictly necessary for the scene, nor draw too much attention to them by placing their façade at the

center of a vista: "Too fond an ostentation of buildings, even of those which are principal, is a common
error."[15] Buildings, in accordance with the principles
of *intricacy*, will always seem more picturesque when
seen obliquely and partly hidden by trees. And it is
important to preserve the unity of the whole scene
by "guarding against the independence to which it [a
building] is naturally prone, and by which an object,
which ought to be part of the whole, is reduced to a
mere individual."[16]

The unity of a garden is more pictorial than it is
architectural. That is the gist of Horace Walpole's praise
of William Kent in his *Essay on Modern Gardening*,
which he included, not insignificantly, in his *Anecdotes
of Painting*: "His buildings, his seats, his temples, were
more the work of his pencil than of his compasses."[17]
The provocations by Price or Knight push to the extreme
an evolution that had already been proclaimed by more
measured minds, and render explicit the power that
gives the art of appearances its privileges over the art
of "sensible truths." When Price evokes Wouwerman's
dung-cart painting, it is in order to underline the impo-
tence of sculpture, the fact that it cannot achieve the
same thing as the painting: it cannot transform a slightly
unsavory subject into a source of pleasure for everyone.
The same dung-cart represented in marble, by the most
skilled artist, would yield a detestable work.

We might see there a new contribution to an old
debate about the comparative powers of the mimetic
arts. Two famous lines by Boileau read: "There is no
serpent or odious monster / That imitated by art cannot
be pleasing to our eyes." It is true that he was not talking
about dunghills. Lessing, however, shows that Boileau's

formula is wrong: according to him, the serpents crushing Laocoon can only please the eye if the sculptor refrains from translating into the stone the expressions of horror present in Virgil's verses. But there is something more at stake in the privilege Lessing gives to the art of "sensible appearances" over the art that carves ideas into hard stone. More than underlining the fact that the two arts are not equal in their ability to produce works that are pleasing to the eye, what Lessing does is posit the virtue of an art that is specifically of the gaze. The painter is first and foremost an artist of the gaze, a person who can individualize – in an indecisive extension and in the shifting spectacle of fields and woods, hills and ponds – a specific dramaturgy of contrasting appearances that fuse into a unified whole. A sculpture of the dung-cart would be repugnant or grotesque because we would see in it the desire to realize an idea in stone, and we would grasp the poverty of the idea through its bizarre rendition. The painter, conversely, does not translate an idea onto the canvas. His gaze seizes a play of appearances, and his canvas prolongs the effects of that play toward another artistic gaze. What is created in the alliance between the appearances of the canvas and the real of the art of gardening, or of the journey across mountains and lakes, is another idea of art. According to this new idea, art is less concerned with producing forms, and more concerned with forging a way of seeing and feeling that extends the sympathy of illusions and movements that was then being designated by the word nature. It is less about defining the criteria of artistic perfection, and more about the principles of an aesthetic education – an expression that, in that same period, became the title of a famous series of essays by Schiller.

That is the transformation that took place in the years since the Abbé Dubos opposed mechanical imitation, with its exact reproduction of the form of a farmer on a country road, and artistic imitation, which alone touches the heart because it captures nature in the only place where it can truly manifest itself: in the drama of human passions translated into the expressions of the characters. The wooded roads used by farmers, the trees that line those roads, and the ponds they skirt now have their own *character*. This character is itself a singular aspect of a nature that composes a unified effect in a specific frame insofar as its power exceeds that frame. The artist is the person who feels this power, and transmits it to others. There is no need to set a pathetic scene in the foreground to do that. Painters, in fact, had already refuted the arguments offered by the theoreticians of *mimesis*. They had shown that the entirety of nature was already present in the drama composed by the trees of a forest, the flowing waters of a stream, the still waters of a lake – as well as by promontories, river embankments, passing clouds, shafts of light, or gusts of wind. Nature is there, at once condensed into a scene and exceeding its limits, for anyone who can not only see it, but feel it.

No one has expressed the power of this feeling that exceeds sight better than Gilpin, whose descriptions of his travels through the lakes and mountains of Cumberland combine the precise gaze of the watercolor artist with the enthusiasm of a servant of God before the spectacle of creation. What serves henceforward as the norm for art is the "living scene" – the scene painted by nature itself, for which the lines of a poem or the strokes of a brush will never be more than "gross, insipid substitutes." This is so because "we may be pleased with the description, and the picture: but the soul can *feel* neither, unless the force of our own imagination aid the poet's, or the painter's art; exalt the idea; and *picture things unseen.*"[18] We might think that these lines simply point to the gap already underlined by the Abbé Dubos between the art that pleases through simple imitation, and the art in which we are touched by the power of nature. The difference is that the status of the gap has changed. It is no longer a matter of pitting a low genre, which copies a vulgar nature, against an elevated genre, which imitates an ideal nature. The gap defines a deficiency constitutive of art in the face of a nature whose singular power – the power of connection – no longer allows itself to be divided into a noble and a low genre. The very powerlessness of art, however, is also what summons forth the power that compensates for it. That power is called the imagination. Not the imagination of the artist who invents subjects and composes scenes according to the norms of an ideal nature, but the imagination of the spectator who must feel and translate, in his turn, the power of a nature that flits across the frame that encloses its representations. Art escapes its powerlessness insofar as it can use it to elicit the power that completes it. That, undoubtedly, is what causes the unhappiness of the sculptor: his work is "perfect" as a product of art. It is fully contained in the realized idea that it puts on display. The perfection of painting, for its part, is that of an imperfect art that cannot close in on itself: it points to a nature whose power it can only suggest, and that never completes itself in any particular form. The art of painting exerts this perfection of the imperfect at its best in those instances when its procedures announce themselves as sketches to be completed in order to arrive at a representation that is merely suggested. Gilpin writes:

> Hence it perhaps follows, that the perfection of the art of painting is not so much attained by an endeavour to form an exact resemblance of nature in a *nice representation of all her minute parts*, which we consider as almost impracticable, ending generally in flatness, and insipidity; as by aiming to give those bold, those strong characteristic touches, which excite the imagination; and lead it to form half a picture itself.[19]

This, too, led to an upheaval in the hierarchy of genres. "Hence it is that even a rough sketch, by the hand of a master, will often strike the imagination beyond the most finished work."[20] And inferior genres, such as paintings of landscapes, flowers, or animals, usually offer more material for the work of the imagination than the more elevated genre of history painting. The art of sensible appearances follows the movement of a nature that already operates of its own accord by "bold" and "strong" touches that suggest the agency of a totality, one that can be felt everywhere without ever being given anywhere. The virtue of painting is to draw sketches of this – not given – totality, and to engage the power of the imagination, which goes beyond what the eye sees and projects itself past what is given. That is why Gilpin cannot accept the reasons, restrictive as always, that Burke gives to explain the preference for the sketch over the finished work: "*The imagination*, says he, *is entertained with the promise of something more; and does not acquiesce in the present object of the sense.*"[21] Gilpin replies that it is not a question of "*promise*," but of reality. The bare walls and the scaffolding of a building under construction certainly promise a home to come, but they do not "entertain" the imagination. The imagination is entertained when its power to positively *create* something new is set in motion. To create something, though not as the vague reverie elicited by the landscape or the canvas, but as the work that they demand, the work that "exalts the idea" by making the unseen visible. The idea to be exalted is not that which presides over the realization of a work like the blueprint for a building or the sketch for a sculpture. Pausing over the spectacle of light and shadow, whether on a fine evening in nature or on the canvas of a painter, reverses the path of *mimesis*. The idea that matters now is the one that comes after: the idea announced by the sketches of nature or of the art of appearances, but surrendered to the only power capable of completing it by going beyond what they offer to sight. The imagination no longer goes from the idea to the form that realizes it. Instead, it goes from the experienced effect toward its still-indeterminate idea. Is it not this reversal that Kant records with the notion of a purposiveness without a purpose?

IV
Beyond the Visible

Unity in variety. That is the classical criterion of beauty that the art of gardening is constantly being reminded to heed. And the notion of the picturesque appears to satisfy that criterion perfectly. If the painter's work is to equal nature, he must introduce into his canvas an exact proportion of varied traits, and fuse them into a harmonious whole. But that also means that a painting is always balanced on an edge, since the variety that attracts the gaze must also lose itself in the unity that takes it beyond itself.

This tension between unity and variety is already present in the definition of intricacy, the preeminent criterion of the picturesque. Intricacy does not mean simply that everything has to merge; it also demands that something should elude the gaze. Price is faithful to Hogarth's idea when he defines intricacy as "that disposition of objects which, by a partial and uncertain concealment, excites and nourishes curiosity."[1] Price wants to oppose this "curiosity" to the monotony of Brown's smooth and undulating gardens. But all improvers, be they disciples or detractors of Brown, share the same fundamental principle, which can be expressed thus: the gaze must be bounded in a way that does not allow it to see the limit of what it is looking at. There must be a limit that conceals the limit. Whately lays bare this principle better than anyone else: the view of a vast expanse of water holds no attraction for the eye, unless it can find a fixed point upon which to rest.[2] It is preferable, then, for the banks of a lake to be visible. But a landscape whose elements are all given to sight leave nothing for the imagination to do, and so the very banks that give sight an anchoring point must themselves dissimulate the limits of the lake's expanse. For that reason, and depending on the case, it is advisable to lower the banks: that way, the lapping waters on the surface allow the viewer to think that the shore is still off in the distance. Or, on the contrary, to raise the banks, making sure that there are parts that "retire" and "advance," and to use the "screens" provided by the vegetation to give the idea that the lake extends beyond sight. In this way, "the extent may be kept in uncertainty; a hill or a wood may conceal one of the extremities, and the country beyond it, in such a manner, as to leave room for the supposed continuation of so large a body of water. (...) [T]he scene is closed, but the extent of the lake is undetermined; a complete form is exhibited to the eye, while a boundless range is left open to the imagination."[3] That is the principle that Kent, and then Brown, applied to the park at Stowe to thwart the "formality" of the park originally designed by Bridgeman. The view of the "Temple of Kent" thus opens onto a number of limitations that create the sense of boundlessness: the Temple of Bacchus, once too exposed, is now partially obscured by trees; the woods on the top of the hill and along one of its sides seem deep, and high; the lawn is vast, but a part of its boundary, artfully concealed, suggests the idea of a still vaster space; lastly, one sees only a small part of the lake, whose extremities are also concealed so as not to diminish its grandeur in the imagination.[4] The very same principle was applied to the lake of the newly conceived park at Painshill: because of its form, of the disposition of some islands, and of the trees on them and on the banks, the lake "always seems to be larger than it is."[5] That same principle, we recall, is what accounts for the majesty of the waterfall at Leasowes despite its modest water volume: the deft dissimulation of the "height from whence it flows" allowed the gaze to confer upon the scene a grandeur that exceeds its dimensions.

We must not misunderstand the reach of these precepts. They are not mere artifices designed to enlarge, in the imagination, bodies of water or lawns of modest dimensions. The point is not so much to increase dimensions as to separate two types of magnitude: the aesthetic magnitude of the scene and the mathematical magnitude of the objects that compose it. It was Kant who went on to formalize this distinction between two types of magnitude. That said, the distinction could already be deduced from Hogarth's analysis, and was central not only to the principles established by the improvers, which Whately formalized for their art, but also to what Gilpin sees unfolding on the vast theater of wild nature. Art's perfection is akin to the power of nature, and consists in the appearance of this magnitude that splits itself off from the reality of mathematical dimensions. The history of aesthetics after Kant has kept only the duality between the beautiful and the sublime, but at the price of ignoring the two intermediary notions that the art of gardening and the description of landscapes had used to construct their own poetics: the *picturesque* and the *grand*.

To understand the role played by these two notions, we must revisit the book that cast its shadow over all the reflections and descriptions of the theoreticians of the art of gardening, and of the picturesque journey: Burke's *A Philosophical Enquiry into the Origins of Our Ideas of the Sublime and Beautiful*. Burke creates a chasm between the sublime and the beautiful, while at the same time giving each of those sentiments a restrictive principle. He links the notion of beauty to smallness: "Beautiful objects small" is the title of one of the sections of his book. And yet, instead of demonstrating that proposition with a concrete illustration, Burke relies on the linguistic use of diminutive epithets for the people one loves and for domestic animals.[6] The more concrete qualities of smoothness and delicacy, which he associates with the principle of insensible variation, are themselves connected to the privilege of the small. Burke thus denies beauty to the "robust trees of the forest," which were so dear to landscape architects, but grants it to the myrtle, the orange tree, the jessamine, and the vine,[7] all of which are more appropriate to the French or Dutch gardens that Burke himself criticizes for their rectilinear proportions. The sublime, for its part, is certainly grand, but its grandeur is defined by the debasement experienced by those affected by it. The sublime's most salient causes are power, terror, darkness, and privation. Burke, it is true, adds the sentiment of infinity to this list, but he does so in order to connect its experience to the principle of insensible variation. The nobility of "rotunds," he says, depends on the fact that "you can no longer fix a boundary; turn which way you will, the same object still seems to continue, and the imagination has no rest."[8] But Burke understands this work of the imagination through a restrictive category, that of deceit: "A true artist should put a generous deceit on the spectators, and effect the noblest design by easy methods. [...] No work of art can be great, but as it deceives; to be otherwise is the prerogative of nature only."[9]

The unstated counterpart to Burke's claim is that nature is not an artist, because it does not deceive. It is precisely on this point that even the authors who rely on Burke's analyses break from the presuppositions that inform them. Gilpin echoes Burke when he says that painting "is the *art of deceiving*; and its great perfection lies in the exercise of this art."[10] Gilpin's point, however, is that such deception is the means that painting uses to align itself with the "grand style" that nature itself uses to paint its scenes. Because nature, too, is an artist through its art of dissimulation: it confuses the lines of mountains; it avails itself of the confusion to hide the insularity of an island; it renders what is distant indistinct, or hides the base and the peaks of mountains in fog; it uses the variety of rocks and scree scattered along its slopes to create a grandiose unity, and the seeming uniformity of a circular lake to reflect the diversity of surrounding peaks. Sometimes, nature even renders uncertain the distinction between the reflection and the reflected object. That is the extraordinary illusion that the Genevese Jean-André de Luc experienced on the paths of Mount Chaumont that overlook Lake Neuchâtel:

The lake's surface was so placid that it reflected the blue of the sky as if it were the sky itself. The trees on the slopes below the path stretched their leaves beyond the horizon before us, thus hiding the land on the opposite shore as well as the mountains. But between the trunks we could see the lake, while above the branches we glimpsed the sky; and the color of both one and the other was so completely the same that it seemed, as long as nothing happened to destroy the illusion, as if we were floating on a small satellite through boundless space.[11]

Nature is much stronger at creating illusions than the landscapists at Stowe or Painshill, because nature erases the most radical border: the one that separates appearance from reality. But this illusion can no longer be assimilated to the dissimulation designed to seduce an imagination that is always willing to let itself be deceived. Instead, it is now a power that exceeds the qualities specific to producing predetermined effects, a power that engages the work of the imagination and casts the mind itself out of its usual proportions.

The picturesque tends toward its own overcoming, toward a state in which the happy combination of varied objects is abolished in a holistic effect: the *grandeur* that reduces this variety to a unity that neutralizes the individuality of the objects and their qualities. The same process erases likewise the usual link between cause and effect, according to which a particular spectacle produces the corresponding effects of pleasure or pain. This is how Burke's criteria become blurry: the smooth surface of a lake is prised away from the simple "smallness" of beauty, and the desolate surface of a mountain covered by enormous boulders from the simple "terror" of the sublime. Both one and the other meet in the same effect of "grandeur," and this "grandeur" produces a specific effect: rather than the landscape seeming vaster than it actually is, it is now the mind that is enlarged. The way travelers describe it, this enlarging of the mind first manifests itself in a state of stupor and unnamable happiness. This state exceeds the pleasure the eye derives from agreeably varied spectacles, but does not confuse itself with the terror experienced at the sight of menacing spectacles. The Archbishop Thomas Herring, a colleague of pastor Gilpin, wrote about this new sentiment following a journey to the wild mountains of Wales:

> The face of it [the mountain] is grand and bespeaks the magnificence of nature, and enlarged my mind so much, in the same manner as the stupendousness of the ocean does, that it was some time before I could be reconciled to the level counties. Their beauties were all of the littlest; and, I am afraid, if I had seen Stowe in my way home, I should have thrown some unmannerly reflections upon it; I should have smiled at all the little niceties of art, and beheld with contempt an artificial ruin, after I had been agreeably terrified with something like the rubbish of creation.[12]

The agreeable terror Herring evokes here belongs to Burke's lexicon. But the "enlargement" of the mind thus seized by contradictory feelings calls into question the "smallness" to which Burke had confined beauty. It also defines a configuration of the mind that leaves behind not only the distinctions Burke draws between psychic states, but his entire psychology. What is being described in the passage is a state in which the indeterminacy of contraries leads the mind to discover sensible powers that cannot be framed by the usual descriptive terms. Gilpin likewise shows how an "extraordinary circumstance" – whether of calm or storm – produces a similar state of union of contraries: a calm enthusiasm that suspends the normal use of our mental powers. Here, once again, nature-as-artist surpasses art in its ability to produce illusions: "If an artificial mirror, a few inches long, placed opposite to a door, or a window, produces often very pleasing reflections; how noble must be the appearance, when an area of many leagues in circumference is formed into one vast mirror; and this mirror surrounded by a combination of great, and beautiful objects? The majestic repose of so grand, so solemn, and splendid a scene raises in the mind a sort of enthusiastic calm, which spreads a mild complacence over the breast – a tranquil pause of mental operation, which may be felt, but not described."[13] What produces this state of suspension is a general, indistinct power that leads objects to lose their individuality and qualities. It is only after the mind has been transported by this general impression that it can detail its elements: the mirror-like lake, the purity of the elements, the hues of the mountains, and the variety of the reflections. But the effect itself could only be felt through the neutralization of those qualities that we would be able to designate as its causes.

That explains why the same effect of transport and suspension can be produced by an effect that is in every way opposed to that of the lake-become-mirror: "When we take a view of such a glorious scene in all its splendor, we regret, that it should ever be deformed by the rough blasts of *tempest*: and yet I know not, whether, under this latter circumstance, it may not have a still greater *power over the imagination*. Every little idea is lost in the wild uproar and confusion of such a scene."[14] What is also lost in the global effect are the specific elements that compose the scene. It is of course possible to describe the broken clouds drifting across the sky, the mountains half-obscured by atmospheric vapors, the trees straining under the blast of a tempest, the lake stirred from the bottom and whitening the rocky promontory with its foam. It is likewise possible to evoke one or another circumstance capable of giving the scene even more intensity: "In the midst of the tempest, if a bright sunbeam should suddenly break out; and in Shakespear's language, *light up the storm,* the scenery of an agitated lake, thus assisted by the powers of contrast, affects both the *imagination,* and the *eye,* in a still greater degree."[15] But if the clouds and flashes of lightning stand out and produce "sublime ideas," it is because they orchestrate the disappearance of the particularity of the objects in the selfsame global sentiment. The storm "leads the eye, in its pursuit of *objects,* to the *grandeur of the effect.*"[16] That is why the vast and solitary expanses of the Helvellyn – where stones are sometimes scattered carelessly over its surfaces, and sometimes appear shivering in cascades of crumbling fragments – produce the same effect as the calm waters of the lake: by fusing into the same whole, they too "distend the mind, and fix it in a kind of stupor."[17] Doctor Johnson is indeed quite wrong when he deems the barren mountains of the Scottish Highlands to be devoid of form. It is true that none of them offers the flowery pastures and waving harvests that he liked, but its "form as a mountain is unquestionably grand and sublime in the highest degree. For that poverty in objects, or *simplicity,* as it may be called, which no doubt injures the beauty of a Scotch landscape; is certainly at the same time the *source of sublimity*."[18]

Simplicity is not just the state in which variety is erased for the sake of unity. It is also the state in which that unity constitutes a self-sufficient totality. Confronted by the sublime spectacle, the imagination is no longer called upon to play the role of artist by adding what the painting lacks. Instead, it is called upon to conceive itself, and to push the mind to conceive itself, as other, as transported elsewhere before the spectacle of a plenitude that lacks nothing. Far from the terror and humiliation that Burke invokes, there is something glorious in the calm experience of this grandeur where extreme wealth and extreme poverty are equal. The spectacle of the sublime draws the mind away from its usual regime and makes it the inhabitant of another world.

This transport can take the form of the sense of wonder at a world that has been returned to its primitive state. In Patrick Brydone's account, reaching the summit of Mount Etna at daybreak mimics the creation of the world:

The whole atmosphere by degrees kindled up, and shewed dimly and faintly the boundless prospect around. Both sea and land looked dark and confused, as if only emerging from their original chaos; and light and darkness seemed still undivided; till the morning by degrees advancing, completed the separation. The stars are extinguished, and the shades disappear. The forests, which but now seemed black and bottomless gulphs, from whence no ray was reflected to shew their form or colours, appear a new creation rising to the sight; catching life and beauty from every increasing beam. The scene still enlarges, and the horizon seems to widen and expand itself on all sides: 'till the sun, like the great Creator, appears in the east, and with his plastic ray completes the mighty scene. All appears enchantment; and it is with difficulty we can believe we are still on earth. The senses, unaccustomed to the sublimity of such a scene, are bewildered and confounded; and it is not till after some time, that they are capable of separating and judging of the objects that compose it.[19]

We do not know if, in England, Brydone had seen Salvator Rosa's painting of Empedocles' death. But it is clear that the figure and legend of that philosopher throwing himself into the furnace of the volcano weaves its way into the memory of the Bible to compose this scene of the origin of the world. Jean-André de Luc offers a more peaceful description of the "feeling of being in paradise" that took hold of him and of his traveling companion during the two hours they spent sitting silently side-by-side and contemplating Lake Neuchâtel from Mount Chaumont: "It had been so long since the air had circulated so imperceptibly in her lungs, so long since she had felt, as she did at that moment, no hunger, thirst, disgust, cold, warmth, weakness, no need to move or rest, no fear or desire – other than the desire to remain forever in this state."[20] This state, which neutralizes ordinary sensations and feelings, inevitably reminds the Genevese de Luc of the feelings that Saint-Preux expresses about the mountains of the Valais, where,

> in the purity of the air where I found myself, I came to
> an understanding of the genuine cause of my change of
> humor, and of the return of that inner peace I for so long

had lost. Indeed, it is a general impression experienced by all men, although they do not all notice it, that high in the mountains where the air is pure and subtle, one breathes more freely, one feels lighter in the body, more serene of mind; pleasures there are less intense, passions more moderate. Meditations there take on an indescribably grand and sublime character, in proportion with the objects that strike us, an indescribably tranquil delight that has nothing acrid or sensual about it. It seems that by rising above the habitation of men one leaves all base and earthly sentiments behind, and in proportion as one approaches ethereal spaces the soul contracts something of their inalterable purity. There, one is grave without melancholy, peaceful without indolence, content to be and to think.[21]

In the *Theory of Garden Art*, the definitive treatment of the subject in Kant's day in Germany, Hirschfeld cites at length Brydone's cosmogonical vision, as well as Rousseau's and de Luc's more peaceful versions, in order to illustrate the idea that the sublime is a calm elevation that lifts us above the circumstances of ordinary life:

How much the entirety of the soul expands, exerting all its strength, laboring to encompass everything when a vista to the ocean opens before us, or when on a bright winter's night the infinity of creation filled with radiant planets and burning fixed stars seems to unfold before our eyes! Mankind's love of greatness, which points to our loftier purpose, is so powerful and unmistakable that it can no longer be denied. The enjoyment of greatness provides the mind and imagination with nourishment that brings complete contentedness; the individual rises above the lowly common perspective to a higher realm of images and sensations; he feels that he is no longer mundane but rather a creature empowered to tower high above where we stand.[22]

In this way, lovers of painting, theoreticians of the picturesque garden, and travelers in love with grandiose landscapes created a series of transitions that fill the gap that Burke had established between the smallness of the beautiful and the terror of the sublime. The picturesque introduced its ruptures and ruggedness into the beauty of varied lines. And, inversely, grandeur fused the ruggedness or desolation of landscapes, as well as the calm solemnity or impetuous violence of the elements, into the unity of a common feeling of elevation that draws man out of his ordinary situation and teaches him his "loftier purpose." Kant inherited this slow elaboration, just as he inherited the links that had been forged between the art of gardening and the art of painting. But if he develops his analysis of the sublime around the descriptions of mountains, boulders, seas, and storms through which those lovers, theoreticians, and travelers had constituted the landscape of the sublime, it is the better to erase the landscape of thought that they had connected to it. It is in order to re-establish Burke's brutal polarity and to link, once again, the sublime to a feeling of powerlessness and humiliation. It is here that the ambiguity of Kant's relation to Burke becomes manifest. Kant may claim, a bit arrogantly, that there is a great difference between his "transcendental exposition of aesthetic judgments" and "the physiological one, as worked out by *Burke* and many acute men among us."[23] But his transcendental exposition is only possible at the price of restoring, against the theoreticians of the picturesque and the grand, the dramaturgy of the beautiful and the sublime first formulated by Burke. The Archbishop Herring had given rise to an entire tradition by admiring the "magnificence of nature" where previous generations had seen only the "rubbish of creation." Kant brutally dismisses the sublimity of shapeless mountains and the raging sea, and finds anew the down-to-earth wisdom of Doctor Johnson when he writes: "Who would apply the term 'sublime' to shapeless mountain masses towering one above the other in wild disorder, with their pyramids of ice, or the dark and tempestuous ocean, or such things?"[24] It will be said that Kant is overstating the point in order to drive home the fact that the sublime is not in the crude materiality of the stone or water, but in the mind of the person contemplating them. But the effect of Kant's repatriation of the sublime into the realm of the mind is that it suppresses the direct and consequential relation between the grandeur of the landscape and the enlargement of the mind. It is only by humiliating the rational being that the sublime can lead him to the realization of his own grandeur. The two forms of the sublime that Kant mobilizes employ the same regressive operation with relation to the analyses of the picturesque and the grand. The analysis of the mathematical sublime may call to mind the way that both nature-as-artist and the art of gardening play with apparent and real dimensions. That analysis is clearly based on the difference between mathematical grandeur and aesthetic grandeur. But Kant inverts the meaning of that play by replacing an experience of enlargement with a lesson in powerlessness. For theoreticians of the garden, the imagination experiences an expansion of power when the limits of the field of vision conceal the limits of a lake or forest, or when the oblique position of a building diminishes its real dimensions in order to increase the feeling of its grandeur. In Kant, conversely, what the imagination measures in the face of the basilica or the pyramid – both too large for the imagination to be able to seize them as instantaneous totalities – is its smallness. That obliges the mind as a whole to undergo the violence of an experience of totalization that it cannot complete. However, it is only through the displeasure it thus experiences that the mind discovers, within itself, reason's unconditioned requirement, which demands an intuition of the whole that the gradual progression of the imagination is incapable of supplying. The unfettered work of the imagination becomes in Kant the demonstration of the radical break that separates it from the truly infinite, which is accessible only to reason and which has its place only in the suprasensible universe in which reason must act, but which it cannot dominate through knowledge.

The analysis of the dynamically sublime proceeds along the same lines. It is no longer a question – as it had been for Hirschfeld and for all the ecstatic travelers he cites – of the spectacle of the "infinity of creation" opening up unbounded "before our eyes," and immediately lifting "the individual above the lowly common perspective to a higher realm of images and sensations" that teaches him his "loftier purpose." The sensible spectacle only leads the mind toward the realm of the suprasensible through the path of its humiliation. If overhanging rocks, thunderclouds piling up to the vault of heaven, flashes of lightning, tempestuous oceans, the waterfalls of a mighty river, and the eruption of a volcano elicit the feeling of the sublime, it is not because they are grandiose spectacles that exercise our capacity to share in their grandeur. It is, on the contrary, because they are brutal and chaotic powers that we cannot resist and that threaten to annihilate us. Consequently, the sublime resides entirely in the mind's awareness of a superior power, the power of reason that commands the mind not to be afraid of what frightens it, but rather to feel itself a citizen of the suprasensible world where reason alone imposes its law. This very capacity to overcome fear, however, reduces the grandeur of the sublime, which elevated the mind, to the simple reality of a hostile phenomenon that causes fear and calls forth the power to overmaster it. That is why nature is neither more nor less sublime than war. The nature where a satisfied mind could lose itself – where it could be "content to be and to think," and to feel directly called toward its higher vocation – ultimately takes on the face of the enemy who teaches the mind that it must rise above the world where fear reigns, and venture beyond the limits of the sensible world.

V
Politics of the Landscape

Kant tells us, in sum, that there is no landscape where the mind can read its "loftier purpose" or vocation. It is not insignificant that the book in which Kant formulates this proscription was published in 1790, in the context of the French Revolution. That same year, the young William Wordsworth was on his way toward the sublime landscape of the Alps when he discovered, upon landing in Calais, that he need not travel as far as the Alps to see signs of man's vocation to freedom and equality: they could be seen already in the wind playing on the elms along the roads, in the flowers of town fairs, and in the vines on the slopes that dominate the banks of the Saône.[1] That same year, the author of *A Philosophical Enquiry into the Origin of Our Ideas of the Sublime and Beautiful*, Edmund Burke, in an attempt to dampen the ardor of young enthusiasts, published his *Reflections on the Revolution in France*, in which he accuses French legislators of being "like their ornamental gardeners, forming everything into an exact level."[2] Burke pits against these fanatics of abstract rights and rectilinear gardens the English genius of place and circumstances. Curiously, though, this English genius of place finds itself identified with the setting of Versailles when the philosopher starts bristling at the populace that dragged the king and queen of France out of their natural abode and locked them up in Paris, the city of popular passions. This evocation of the crime of *lèse-majesté* provides the occasion for a delicate recollection in the form of a fleeting vision: "It is now sixteen or seventeen years since I saw the queen of France, then the dauphiness, at Versailles; and surely never lighted on this orb, which she hardly seem'd to touch, a more delightful vision. I saw her just above the horizon, decorating and cheering the elevated sphere she just began to move in, – glittering like the morning-star, full of life, and splendour, and joy."[3] The vision of the morning star rising is, of course, a metaphor. But the imagination superimposes onto this metaphor of the royal star at the beginning of its course the image of a youthful silhouette emerging from the horizon of a park with the smooth and waving curves that Burke was so fond of. If Burke evokes this delicate vision, it is only to underline the contrast between it and the brutal glare of the "new conquering empire of light and reason" committed to dissolving the pleasing illusions which "harmonized the different shades of life, and which, by a bland assimilation, incorporated into politics the sentiments which beautify and soften private society."[4]

In the young and enthusiastic poet as in the wise and horrified old man, the revolution is described, metaphorized, and appreciated in one and the same play of references: the new political order is like a landscape. It is a matter of straight or curving lines, of elements that "advance" and "retire," of the play of light and clouds on trees and bodies of water, of unbounded and bounded horizons. In sum, it is a matter of intricacy. That said, the poet and the wise man see things quite differently. In the deep and majestic valleys through which the river cuts its winding path, and on the slopes dotted with farms and orchards, the young man sees a landscape of freedom in harmony with the curves of nature, the rustling of the wind on the trees, and the play of light and shadow on the products of human labor. In other words, he recognizes the charms of Burke's serpentine line and smoothed contours in the countryside of Republican France. Burke, however, in his "letter to a gentleman in Paris," offers a different view of the relation between the landscape and politics: what he sees in the abstract territory constructed by revolutionary laws is the end of the softened curves and the play of light and shadow that had given harmony to the social landscape. He sees the disappearance of a society that was "natural" precisely because it had been constructed slowly and in conformity with the forms of intricacy that give the landscape a unity founded on variety itself: this "mixed system of opinion and sentiment ... which, without confounding ranks, had produced a noble equality, and handed it down through all the gradations of social life."[5] For Burke, the landscape of English freedom is a garden by Capability Brown: its wide open spaces, soft undulations, rounded edges, and insensible variations provided everyone with their unequal share of light and shade. It is the setting of a peaceful social life upon which the nobility and enlightened landowners, heirs to the old chivalry, imprint a character at once majestic and esteemed, much like the clumps formed with tall trees. And it is this setting of English freedom that he superimposes onto the rectilinear parterres of Versailles.

Two ideas of the genius of place, two ways of constructing the natural landscape in a manner hospitable to humans. Two paintings by Gainsborough, one might say. In the first, an elegantly dressed aristocratic figure is surrounded by a landscape, his property, in which a few black dots in the wheat fields or in the meadows are the only indications of the men of the people who find their modest place therein. In the second, a landscape setting that belongs to everyone and to no one, to those who stroll along it and to those who work on it. The topography may be different, but the elms that line French roads and the water that snakes its way through the vines compose a democratic landscape that answers to the wooded settings where the painter depicts farmers going to market on their carts, or their livestock drinking in a pond.

A landscape is the reflection of a social and political order. A social and political order can be described as a landscape. That is the premise that underwrites the images of the poet and the metaphors of the philosopher and statesman. There is a genius of place that animates the landscape and makes it "free." There is a spirit of the laws, an accumulation of ways of being upon which the real force of legislation rests. Nature inspires both one and the other, and each can be a metaphor for the other. For Burke, the tall trees of parks, with their protective shade, symbolize an aristocratic and traditional order that is good for everyone because it is founded on nature, and nature ensures the slow growth of plants and gives each its respective size and place in the whole. For Wordsworth, the garland of flowers on rustic crossroads, maypoles, and republican triumphal arches symbolize a fraternal order based on a nature that generously distributes its goods in equal measure to people who have no desire to rise above others. Evil happens when artifice, the product of human violence, thwarts the free expansion of nature and imposes its *deformities* upon it. That is what the traveler, painter, and pastor William Gilpin summed up when he found himself face-to-face with the untouched landscapes of the Highlands: "Wherever man appears with his tools, deformity follows his steps. His spade, and his plough, his hedge, and his furrow; make shocking encroachments on the simplicity, and elegance of the landscape."[6]

The spade and the plough, the hedge and the furrow: the "tools" that Gilpin mentions indicate what disturbs the beautiful balance envisaged between the harmony of the landscape and social harmony. On the one hand, the spade, that is to say, not just the violence of warriors, but also the power of the state to exercise its legitimate violence; on the other, the plough and the hedge, that is to say, the economy, meaning not just the industrious activity of the people who transform nature, but the property that gives that activity its specific social form. Behind the ideal mediation of mores, which aligns the natural landscape to the social one, there are two powers that give to one the face of exploitation, and to the other the face of domination. This background is at once designated and masked by the notion that is so often used to denounce the despotic violence exerted against the "free" and "natural" arrangement of landscapes and societies: that of *leveling*. The notion was central to the polemics about gardens well before it started being used to express horror at the actions of French revolutionaries. Strangely enough, the very English history of that notion appears to have been forgotten by those who use it. *Levelers*, in fact, was the name given to the rural rebels in the Midlands who destroyed posts and hedges in a rebellion against enclosures in 1607. Then, during the English Civil War, the name was claimed by an organized revolutionary faction whose demands are recorded in a manifesto entitled *An Agreement of the Free People of England* (1649). It seems clear that, by Burke's time, those who denounced the evils of *leveling* had forgotten these "free people" and the upheavals of the English Revolution. That was the price that had to be paid for the elaboration of a specifically English vision of freedom, one founded on a long tradition whose unbroken line of succession bound the forms of a modern constitutional monarchy to the concessions that Magna Carta granted to English barons in 1215. This vision, which Burke systematized, is obliged to make leveling a distinctively French evil. The straight line of French despotism can thus be traced from absolute monarchy to the geometrical and unshaded gardens of Le Nôtre, and from his well-trimmed parterres and hedges to the egalitarian folly of revolutionary legislators with their guillotines. Its counterpart, quite naturally, is to be found in the harmonious continuity between gardens with sinewy paths, a social landscape of "insensible gradations," and the forms of government of a liberal monarchy founded on tradition and willing to empirically accommodate only those novelties that preserve the ancient virtues.

Unfortunately, Brown's gardens – with their isolated clumps, artificial lakes, and vast lawns isolating aristocratic homes – are not particularly well fitted to the idyllic model of protective shades and insensible gradations. If the landowners who paid to have their gardens landscaped sacrificed the charms of intricacy by creating vast vistas, it was precisely in order to better isolate their home by pushing into the far distance any traces of the rustic and laborious life, which was also supposed to enjoy the cover of their benevolent shade. The "liberal" regime of parliamentary monarchy, for its part, yielded to the inegalitarian aspirations of landowners, and did not hesitate to help them in their efforts to erase from the map of the kingdom a form of landscape that was nevertheless bound up with the principle of "insensible gradations," namely the ancient use of commons. The era when improvers undertook their major projects and of polemics over the art of gardening coincided exactly with the last great wave of the enclosures, which were just then starting to impact regions that had more or less eluded them. The resolute intervention of public powers injected new force into that movement, and in so doing acted against their supposed function: to be the guardians of traditional forms of the social balance. It was in fact in the second half of the eighteenth century that the use of "parliamentary enclosure" became widespread. Until then, the introduction of enclosures into the territory of a parish had required consensus, at least in principle. That had meant negotiations on a case-by-case basis, and had often resulted in a portion of the land being set apart for the use of the commons. Now, however, their introduction started to depend on *private acts* of Parliament, which allowed enclosures if there was an agreement between the owners of four-fifths of the lands – that is, an agreement among wealthy landowners. These acts accelerated exponentially in the eighteenth century. Throughout the whole of England, there had been eight private acts of Parliament prior to 1714, eighteen under George I, 229 under George II, and, during the first years of George III's reign, the system expanded to regions that had been preserved until then.[7] The dispossession of poor peasants – small landowners, farmers, or artisans who lost their rights to the use of the land and the multiple products of the "wastes" – became even more noticeable through the process of expanding and remodeling the parks around castles. Some landowners were not satisfied just with cutting down trees and thickets to create the rounded lines of their softly undulating lawns. They also eliminated from the territory of the parish, which sometimes belonged entirely to them, any constructions that obstructed their view. If the homes of the villagers were too close to the manor, they razed those too and moved their inhabitants further away. Lord Harvey, at Ickworth, demolished the hamlet, sparing only the church where his ancestors are buried, because it was too close to the manor. And then he demolished the manor itself in order to build, a little further away, a monumental rotunda whose views would at last not be encumbered by any obstacles. Meanwhile, at Shugborough, Thomas Anson moved the village to trace his park; the following century, his son displaced the village yet again.[8]

The great parks, the wisdom of landowners, and a representative government were supposed to ensure the harmonious gradation of social conditions against the folly of levelers. In reality, though, they did the opposite: they leveled the landscape and wiped out the points of contact and the spaces open to all in order to separate the homes and prerogatives of the rich from the homes and living conditions of a population that they tended to reduce to the same level of poverty. The leveling practice of the rich did meet with opposition, sometimes in the form of petitions, and sometimes in more direct actions, as was the case in West Haddon (Northamptonshire) one August day in 1765. Two artisans invited workers to a football match that, once the crowd had gathered, turned into a bonfire that consumed the fence poles and rails that had been delivered for the construction of an enclosure.[9] The practice was also stigmatized in a poem destined for fame, "The Deserted Village," in which Oliver Goldsmith evokes the obliteration of the landscape of a life at once laborious and joyous: the "never-failing brook, the busy mill," the church that "topt the neighbouring hill," the "hawthorn bush," the "whisperings lovers made" on the "seats beneath the shade," the "sports beneath the spreading tree," the turns at "slights of art and feats of strength," the "dancing pair": all these charms "fled" after the "tyrant's hand" – an "only master" – had seized the cottages, and the avidity of trade had joined hands with the pride of the powerful to produce a desolate landscape whose population was obliged to escape to the cities. The vastness of landscaped parks comes at the expense of this shared space, which had rendered the borders of a property blurry: the paths taken by the poor cut through the lands of the rich, the forest was just as much a supplier of multiple goods for everyone as a space for walks, and the clearing was at once a site for working and for playing. The beautiful open spaces of *improved* gardens have as their complement the physical and symbolic fence that excludes the working population. This is summed up in an engraving, a "before" and "after" diptych ironically entitled *Improvements*. Before: large trees lined the road, shaded the benches where pedestrians could rest, and connected the road both to the commons and to the parks, which could be accessed by means of small ladders. After: the large trees have disappeared and been replaced with tight rows of conifers that rise straight up and whose branches hide the park from view but offer neither shade nor a protective canopy. On the opposite side of the road, the old commons have disappeared and been replaced by a wheat field. And a closed boarded fence lines the sidewalk, now exposed to the sun, where a tired worker is seen walking: after a long day, he has to trek an extra mile to circumvent the park that once upon a time he could cut through to get to his cottage.

Significantly, this diptych is included in one of the chapters of *Fragments on the Theory and the Practice of Landscape Gardening* (1803), published by the most renowned garden architect of the period, Humphry Repton. Indeed, in the *Red Books* that Repton made for his clients, he had the habit of showing off his designs with watercolors of a park before and after his interventions. The perplexing presence of this satirical diptych among images intended as serious illustrations of his practice as an improver shows the art of gardening being confronted by the transformations of the social landscape which are the conditions of that art. Repton appears, in fact, as Capability Brown's heir. He works for the same clientele, and he makes it his job to transform agricultural land into agreeably undulating parks. But he was also an acquaintance of the two great apostles of the picturesque garden, Richard Payne

Knight and Uvedale Price; he knew their texts, and he took the trouble to exchange lengthy letters with Price. Gardens were not a business for Knight and Price: they were content with transforming their own lands and with extracting from their love of painting the elements for a theory of gardening. Unlike Brown and Repton, they were men of letters and art lovers – as well as rich landowners. While this may lead us to look upon their ideas about gardens as purely abstract, we cannot ignore their impact on the wider context, which was defined by two contemporaneous events: the new enclosures, which undercut the model of a society formed as a harmonious landscape of insensible gradations; and the French Revolution, which showed the abyss that could engulf an order of nobles and landowners who had forgotten those "gradations."

It is against this double context that we must understand Knight and Price's call to combine the lessons of painting and those of nature. The link they forge between painting and nature protects their views from the charge that they were pleading for a return to the state of nature that some accused them of – including Repton, who "cannot help seeing a great affinity betwixt deducing gardening from the painter's studies of wild nature, and deducing government from the uncontrolled opinions of man in a savage state."[10] This reproach touches Knight first and foremost: that eccentric had already drawn the reprobation of good society by publishing a work on the scandalous worship of the Priapus. That same good society was quite naturally ready to read Knight's call to "crop th'aspiring larche's saucy head"[11] as an approval of the French guillotine. But that good society should be more attentive to the context of this call: Knight condemns the "unsocial" stinginess of pines in the name of the British genius of soft and curving lines and wide protective branches. The king tree that he pits against the pine is the same great oak that Burke saw as a symbol of the aristocratic order – if, he noted, "you [the aristocracy] are what you ought to be."[12] The tall majestic oak has now become the symbol of a traditional social harmony destroyed by the pride of the nobility and by the stinginess of anti-social trees. All that the supposed cropper of heads does is turn the notions and images of the counterrevolutionary Burke against this social order and landscape, whose masters are clearly not what they "ought to be."

Knight and Price do not dream of a return to the state of nature. Nor do they dream of a rustic and egalitarian republic like the one described by Rousseau's admirer as he stood at the feet of the sublime glaciers of the Grindelwald, and looked upon a landscape of identical houses placed equidistant from each other: emblems of the happiness of a life in which "no one tries to distinguish themselves from, or raise themselves above, others."[13] Richard Payne Knight, the owner of an ironworks, is far from such Swiss dreams of pastoral happiness, and records show that the baronet Uvedale Price demanded more rigorous laws against the farmers and agricultural workers who savagely stripped the trees of his estate. Knight was at first sympathetic to revolutionary ideas and, although he grew disenchanted with them, he remained convinced that the horrors of the Revolution laid the ground that would allow "future times" to see "Just order spring, and genuine liberty," much in the same way as the "currents" that destroy fences ultimately contribute to the fertility of the soil.[14]

Price never shared this enthusiasm, but that made him all the more concerned with ensuring that the new usurpations of property in England would not lead to the same conflagration. The social landscape that Knight and Price plead for is turned toward the past as much as toward the future. Price takes the trouble to articulate the argument: the real "levelers," the people truly responsible for the dangers of the present situation, are the arrogant nobility and the tyrannical improvers whose despotic art upsets the natural configuration of the geographic and social landscape. The only way to combat the revolutionary danger is to restore the state of things prior to this leveling revolution, and that requires restoring more humane forms of ownership, forms that are less disconnected from the world of people who do not own land, less imprinted onto the lines of the landscape, and less emblazoned on how parks are designed. The keywords of a harmonious society are the same as those that define the ideal of the picturesque garden: intricacy and connectivity. If the art of gardening – which is also the art of a sensible use of property – must draw its inspiration from painters, it is because painters look at the world of nature and its inhabitants in a way that differs both from the arrogance of the nobility and from the despotic zeal for uniformity of improvers. The latter, by suppressing the forms of community that cottages, paths, and churches constituted in the landscape of nobiliary property, created "the vacancy of solitary grandeur and power."[15] But painters, and lovers of painting, know that the diversity of objects and figures, and of the links that connect them, is what makes a canvas interesting. They love neither uniform spaces nor the stinginess of enclosures: "Where a despot thinks every person an intruder who enters his domain, and wishes to destroy cottages and pathways, and to reign alone; the lover of painting considers the dwellings, the inhabitants, and the marks of their intercourse, as ornaments to the landscape."[16] Here again, Price's arguments call to mind Gainsborough's rustic scenes, which are the inverse of his aristocratic portraits. These scenes show the influence of Dutch masters by welcoming into the frame not only all the "incidents" of the vegetation, but also farmers with their livestock and carts, a young pig keeper, a farmer's daughter gathering faggots by a pollarded tree, and a large family posing in front of a cottage whose thatched roof is a model of "intricacy." These are images that keep peasant life, rural or wooded spaces without enclosures, and a domestic economy founded on the use of the commons, visible. Burke's aristocratic landscape is thus transposed into the popular setting of a genre painting. Price's quill, however, fuses the incidents and the ruggedness of this rustic universe into a unified tonality that evokes the noble landscapes of Claude Lorrain. The long letter where Price lays bare his principles culminates in a discussion of this tonality, which suffuses the landscape of a peaceful social life. In it, the political lexicon borrowed from Burke is exemplarily transformed into the description of a painting:

> The mutual connection and dependence of all the different ranks and orders of men in this country; the innumerable, but voluntary ties by which they are bound and united to each other, (so different from what are experienced by the subjects of any other monarchy,) are perhaps the firmest securities of its glories, its strength, and its happiness.

Freedom, like the general atmosphere, is diffused through every part, and its steady and settled influence, like that of the atmosphere on a fine evening, gives at once a glowing warmth, and a union to all within its sphere: and although the separation of the different ranks and their gradations, like those of visible objects, is known and ascertained, yet from the beneficial mixture, and frequent intercommunication of high and low, that separation is happily disguised, and does not sensibly operate on the general mind.[17]

The fascinating thing about this passage is not just that it literalizes Burke's metaphors, but that it literalizes them in a very specific way, that is, as the principles of pictorial composition. The gradations of the social order become the shadings of light on the canvas. The dissimulation of inequality in the appearance of the community is treated in the same way as the dissimulation of the furthest edges of a lake or the origin of a waterfall, which give imaginary expansion to a bounded landscape. Even the general tonality of a harmonious society receives its own pictorial identity: it resembles the atmosphere of a fine evening. This atmosphere, we recall, is what characterized a fine evening in nature as equivalent to the warm light of a Claude Lorrain canvas: the landscape was like a painting and the painting like a landscape. Now it is the harmonious coexistence of social classes that is said to be identical to the unity of tone in the painting, which itself resembles the late afternoon light in the countryside – the green English countryside as seen by an eye formed by contemplating the Roman countryside as depicted by the masters.

Price's letter had to prove to his interlocutor the soundness of the thesis that the true art of gardening was deducible from the compositional forms of the masterpieces of the art of painting. If that demonstration never quite got there, it is because it was thrown off track when Price started addressing the lessons of painting to a political art that was then being confronted, due to the violence of recent events, by the most extreme forms of the old problem formulated by Aristotle: how to make the same order of things appear egalitarian to the partisans of equality, and inegalitarian to the partisans of inequality? The solution, Price seems to say, can only be found there where politics imitates the art of gardening, which in its turn imitates the preeminent art of appearances, painting: because that art depicts only the shadows of bodies, it is not obliged to distribute its figures in accordance with the gradations of power or the lines of ownership. When politics strays from this model, when it allows the line that separates "different ranks" to inscribe itself in the common landscape, the bonds of a harmonious society are irremediably broken.

But the demonstration can also lead to another conclusion: painting, and the art of gardening which imitates it, are alone capable of bringing about the peaceful fusion of differences into the same tonality. That is the dream of politics, but politics cannot realize it. After evoking the revolutionary "current" that would fertilize the future, Richard Payne Knight concludes his poem on a much more pacifist note: "May hence ambition's wasteful folly cease, / And cultivate alone the happy arts of peace."[18] Eight years later, after Pitt's England had signed the Treaty of Amiens with France's First Consul, Napoleon Bonaparte, it was Price who confessed in one of his letters: "The only tactics I know, or even wish to know, is that of arranging and disposing trees."[19] The art of gardening thus distributes its effects on two levels: on one, it proposes to concretely arrange a landscape of the visible whose lines are not cut by property; on the other, it contributes to the forms of perception of a common world shared by owners and non-owners. It will be said that this is all about appearances. But, in the age of revolutions, which is also the age of aesthetics, everyone knew that appearance is not the opposite, or the mask, of the real. It is what opens or closes the access to the reality of a common world. Nor is it the product of human artifice and lies, which stand opposite and against the simplicity of nature. It is nature itself that teaches its use and initiates the movement that deploys appearances and their effects. The whole question turns on figuring out where we can fix the destination of this movement, and the ends to which it orients rational beings in an era of storms and tempests sparked by revolutionaries in love with natural reason and rustic simplicity. The ideal of reasonable property fused into the accidents of the landscape that these lovers of painting propose is one way to fix its limits. The same holds for the "painting, in the wide sense,"[20] that Kant discusses in the section where he includes the art of gardening in the classification of the fine arts. This "painting" is an art of making: it extends the lessons of nature from the arrangement of parterres to the forms of sociability, and from the decoration of rooms to the tasteful and unostentatious art of dressing. The power of a free and "irregular" nature is arranged into a diversity where everyone finds their place. But Kant is careful to separate this diversity, which founds a reasonable sociability, from the other form of nature's irregularity: the dark and tempestuous ocean, shapeless mountain masses towering one above the other, and pyramids of ice. De Luc encompassed in one and the same gaze the grandiose glaciers of the Grindelwald and the identical and equidistant houses of a republican village. This political connection between the grandiose mountain and the pastoral and egalitarian village is what Kant splits anew when he retraces a dividing line between the beautiful and the sublime. The pyramids of ice do not provide shelter to any form of communal order. All they do is induce the terror that prompts individuals to find, in themselves, the power that can overcome it: a rational power of freedom that goes beyond nature, and instead of founding one or another form of social community, founds only a kingdom of minds.

Epilogue

In 1790, Kant introduced the art of gardening into the classification of the fine arts by treating it as a branch of painting. Forty years later, Hegel pushed it out by treating it as nothing more than an accessory of architecture. It is true that Hegel did not prepare his *Aesthetics: Lectures on Fine Art* for publication himself: its two volumes were published posthumously. But it was surely Hegel himself who decided on the singular place that the art of gardening occupies in the lectures: he discusses it at the end of the section on the secular architecture of the Middle Ages, which concludes the part devoted to architecture. It seems difficult, however, to deduce the forms of the art of gardening from the principles that govern what Hegel calls "romantic," which is to say Gothic, architecture. Hegel himself makes no effort to connect the art of groves, lawns, and waterfalls to the privilege of subjective interiority which he believes characterizes "romantic" art. Nor does he grant to the art of gardening the role of functioning as the dialectical articulation that leads to the following section, on sculpture. Hegel places the art of gardening at the tail end of the discussion of architecture as if to rid himself of it.

Hegel is of course careful about how he does this. He reintroduces the art of gardening into architecture – that art of objective finality from which Kant extricates it, and, more importantly, from which it had been extricated by its own evolution over the course of the eighteenth century – even though it has nothing to do with Gothic buildings. Significantly, this reintroduction treats the garden as the architectonic extension of a building. The example Hegel chooses to discuss is the park at the Sans Souci palace in Potsdam, whose terraces, rectilinear avenues, parterres, trellises, and pruned hedges could not be further from the "liberality" of English gardens, or from the German imitations of those gardens that Hirschfeld celebrates. Hegel, it must be said, does distinguish between garden architecture, and the art of gardening as such, understood as an art of imitating nature in which the pictorial dimension predominates. But he immediately turns around and disparages the pretensions of the art of gardening to artificially produce a landscaped environment that resembles a natural landscape.

This critique is certainly not specific to the art of gardening. Rather, it fits into the more general framework of Hegel's anti-romantic polemic: the creators of English-style gardens – who try to make it seem as if nature itself had arranged the trees, stones, and bodies of water of a park – resemble those young German poets who exhausted themselves trying to intentionally create a spontaneous poetry. The credo of English landscapists was that they must hide their art, and that was bound to displease the philosopher who believes, on the contrary, that art must show itself first and foremost as the work of spirit. Hegel is clear on this point already in the introduction to the *Lectures on Fine Art*: aesthetics deals only and exclusively with the beauty created by art. Natural beauty exists, of course. But beauty belongs to nature only insofar as nature itself is imbued by the spirit toward which it is destined and which gives it its form. The beauty of nature is the beauty of the living organism, which shows its inner unity in the articulation of its parts, or the beauty of the surface of bodies animated by life, which is their spiritual essence. Kant denied that we can call raging seas or pyramids of ice sublime. Hegel can barely bring himself to admit the idea that we can call a landscape beautiful. A landscape lacks an essential condition of beauty: "Here we have no organic articulation of parts as determined by the Concept and animated into its ideal unity."[1] At around that same time, in a series of gripping lectures delivered to packed halls at the university of Berlin and attended by the philosopher's wife, Alexander von Humboldt set about showing that the connection of impressions and the unity of emotions elicited by a landscape anticipate the scientific understanding of the intimate connection among phenomena.[2] Those lectures gave the savant-turned-artist Gustav Carus the idea for a "latter-day art of landscape" painting that would be like a history of the earth.[3] Hegel, for his part, sees in the contemplation of a landscape only the relationship between two exteriorities: a diversity of objects (the silhouettes of mountains, meandering streams, clusters of trees, various habitations) on one side, and, on the other, an encompassing feeling that invests these disparate figures with nothing more than the subjective and empirical unity of an attractive or imposing spectacle.

Differently put, there is no nature-as-artist creating scenes, no art that prolongs the effects of nature's broad strokes, and no imagination that completes the painting they outline. As for those spectacles of grandeur – the starry heaven, the stillness of a moonlit night, the peace of a meandering stream, the tempestuous ocean – that transport spirit beyond its usual domain, they only move the spirit insofar as it recognizes in them analogies of its own states. The relation of a landscape to a mental state is akin to that which transforms animals into symbols of courage, strength, or cunning.[4] Gilpin saw nature's supreme art in the calm lake that reflects the ruggedness of the surrounding mountains like a mirror. For Hegel, art only begins with the gesture of the child who throws stones into a river and marvels at the circles that result from his action.[5] In the materials of nature that it borrows and in the forms that it reproduces – like the arborescence of Gothic arcs, which seem to connect as if by chance – spirit sees only itself. What we call the imitation of nature is nothing other than the spirit's expression of its own activity. Even in the passages where Hegel celebrates the "prose of life" illustrated by Dutch painters, the examples he gives are not Ruysdael, Berchem, or Hobbema, or landscapes, forests, and brooks, but instances of human activity: "Velvet, metallic lustre, light, horses, servants, old women, peasants blowing smoke from cutty pipes, the glitter of wine in a transparent glass, chaps in dirty jackets playing with old cards."[6] It will be said that spirit, that negator of solid materiality, enjoys seeing its own work in the simple appearance of objects whose material execution often requires substantial efforts. But the point remains that it is in the representation of these manifestations and objects of human activity that it finds pleasure, and not in the light of the moon reflected on the sea, snowcapped mountains, or the pink and orange clouds painted by Caspar David Friedrich, Johan Christian Dahl, or Gustav Carus. Distant as Hegel is from the theoreticians of mimesis, he adopts their point of view: the value of a painting is not in the spectacle of earth, sky, and water, but in its representation of human activity. It is there and only there that they saw the imitation of real nature. What Hegel sees there, for his part, is the expression of spirit, whose most mediocre realizations will always prevail over the most beautiful spectacles of nature.

Spirit only ever sees itself, even if that means seeing itself through imperfect eyes or unskilled hands, even if that means no longer seeing itself in any visible form. That is the radical transformation that the concept of the sublime undergoes in Hegel. The sublime is no longer the feeling of exaltation that the mind experiences before a calm lake reflecting the sky like a mirror, or before waters made turbulent and rough by storm. It is no longer the mark of the inferiority that the mind feels when confronted by infinite grandeur, or by nature's irresistible power – even if that feeling of inferiority leads to the subsequent discovery of its own grandeur. The sublime is neither a property of the spectacle of nature, nor its effect, whether direct or indirect. It is, exclusively, an artistic category. And, in that framework, the sublime is a family affair that is always played out between spirit and itself. It is spirit that finds itself lacking in relation to itself, in relation to the spiritual content that it must clarify and express. Sublime art is the art in which the spiritual meaning cannot be depicted in any visible form. The exemplary form of its existence is the sacred text, which expresses a divine unity that cannot be captured in any phenomenal form.

Nature is neither an artist creating beauty, nor the sublime manifestation of a divine reason. Long gone are the days when the young Hegel, raising his eyes to the eternal vault of heaven and the brilliant moon, felt his sense slipping away as he abandoned himself to the pantheistic power of the incommensurable.[7] In the intervening years, of course, he had had to ponder the fate of his poem's addressee, Friedrich Hölderlin. Two years after Hegel wrote "Eleusis," Hölderlin wrote a tragedy about Empedocles, a divine man who, before plunging into the crater of Mount Etna, taught the Agrigentians to forget the laws and customs that had been handed down to them so that they could look at divine nature like newborns, allowing themselves to be lulled by its sacred chant and pledging before its noble forces the oath of living as a free and equal people.[8] Five years later, Schelling saw firsthand the sad spectacle of the poet returning from France "in a state of total mental absence."[9] Long before the lectures on fine art, Hegel had already said his goodbyes to this sublime nature, which overwhelms spirit, but also gives a lesson in community. In the lectures, however, even the gentle curves of English gardens and their modest efforts to erase the hard lines of property from the landscape are cast aside. And the entire movement that had brought the art of gardening into the liberal arts is thus dismissed. Hegel returns that art to an auxiliary role. It has no lessons to teach about nature, only about the art of using its products to agreeably expand the perimeters of homes: "A garden as such should provide no more than cheerful surroundings, i.e. surroundings merely, worth nothing in themselves and so never distracting us from human affairs and our inner life. Here architecture with its mathematical lines, with its order, regularity, and symmetry has its place and orders natural objects themselves architecturally."[10] Architecture, order, regularity, symmetry: Hegel methodically restores all the authoritarian principles that both the art of gardening and nature enthusiasts had spent a century freeing themselves from. It is only logical, therefore, that the brief excursus Hegel devotes to this art should conclude with him praising the monarchic model that had brought those principles to perfection:

> But the architectural principle has been carried furthest in French horticulture, where gardens are usually attached to great palaces; trees are planted in a strict order beside one another in long avenues, they are trimmed, and real walls are formed from cut hedges; and in this way nature itself is transformed into a vast residence under the open sky.[11]

This is how the art of landscape gardening, so recently introduced into the kingdom of the fine arts, found itself expelled from that kingdom. And nature – or, at least, a certain idea of nature – was expelled along with it. Nature had been an intruder in that kingdom ever since it divested itself of its role as an ideal by assuming the shape of forests and mountains, of calm or tumultuous waters, of starry skies and morning or evening clouds. Through its indiscreet presence, nature had insidiously undermined the foundations of the representative edifice – indeed, it had blurred all the borders around which it was structured: not only had it confounded the roles of model and copy, but also of artwork and artist. And if nature placed itself in the position of artist, it was the better to undermine that position: nature was an artist as long as it was not one, as long as the spectacles it created were not the realization of the desire to make art. With nature-as-artist, the very difference between art and the absence of art was undone. And that is certainly more than any system of the fine arts can tolerate.

Still, this incompatibility can be read backwards, as it were. By occupying and confounding the places of model and copy, artwork and artist, artist and non-artist, nature, as understood by the creators of gardens and landscape enthusiasts, had undone the rickety arrangement of equivocal notions that had lent its norms to the fine arts, starting with the very notion of the "imitation of nature." One could, of course, try to shore up the edifice anew by pushing nature aside, and by claiming that art does not imitate an external reality, that art is exclusively a matter of spirit, and that spirit only ever recognizes its own image in its works. That is what Hegel does when he pushes the nature of English landscapists and German dreamers out of the realm of art. Some will want to read in that gesture the birth of an art that is, at long last, "autonomous." But the very opposite is the case, because something had entered art – and the "spirit" it expresses – with that nature, something that would not leave it, and that would thenceforward be constitutive of art: non-art, that is to say, the indistinction between art and non-art. In effect, the art freed from nature that Hegel celebrates is not the pure expression of the spirit of artists. It is, rather, the product of a collective form of life that has the exact same characteristic as the nature that he had expelled: it, too, makes art without making it. The price spirit must pay to affirm its supremacy is the distance that separates it from its own manifestations.

Hegel resolves the problem by confining this art/form of life, whose creators did not quite know what they were doing, to the past, to a time when spirit searched for itself in the exteriority of matter. But, he says, from now on spirit will find itself without passing through that detour. That is why art is a thing of the past. It was not long, however, before posterity reversed the argument: art is not a thing of the past. Art is present wherever spirit is still searching for itself. There is art wherever the spirit of a burgeoning form of life needs to give itself a shape, wherever spirit must seek out the elements of this figuration in the most prosaic reality and make of the figure thus constructed the means for transforming that very reality. Hegel's *Aesthetics: Lectures on Fine Art* was published in Berlin in 1835. Six years later, in Boston, an American reader of Hegel, Ralph Waldo Emerson, outlined the task of the poet to come: to give spiritual expression to the form of life of this new American world whose poetry is still latent, still hidden in the banality of domestic activities, in the crassness of economic relations, and in the brutality of conflicts. Not long after, Ruskin confronted the prettiness of easel painting with the spiritual value of an art of building and decorating habitations designed to provide shelter and express life. The following century, the artists of revolutionary Russia would declare that the role of art is no longer to make "artworks" but to construct the forms of a new life and to transform the entire setting of the visible – from the buildings intended for the Communist International to propaganda kiosks, posters, and street signs – so as to make it the sensible appearance of a world without property.

What made this project possible is that, meanwhile, a new force for transforming the world had established itself: technique. But its role is all too often misunderstood. It is seen as the force that imposes the supremacy of spirit, which dictates its will to nature instead of trying to imitate it. And it is indeed in those terms that Hegel celebrates it when he writes that "the discovery of any insignificant technical product has higher value, and man can be prouder of having invented the hammer, the nail, etc., than of manufacturing tricks of imitation."[12] But technique is not simply the force that tames nature. It is also the power that, like an understudy, took over nature's role as the representative, in art, of non-artistic life. Uvedale Price tried to find images of the continuity between the scenes of nature and the constructions of human art in Claude Lorrain's landscapes; that continuity would be realized, in the time of Frank Lloyd Wright, thanks to the new resources offered by concrete, glass, and steel. That was still in the distant future in 1835, the year Hegel's *Aesthetics* was published in Berlin. And yet, even then, technique had already started to blur the reference points of nature and art. That same year, Gustav Carus was passing through Paris, where he observed that, when it came to "tricks of imitation," technique was able to attain a level of perfection unavailable to the painter's hand: Daguerre's dioramas could in fact reproduce not just the forms and colors of a building or landscape, but also the variations in their aspects depending on the light and hours of the day.[13] Three years later, the same Carus was alerted by his friend Alexander von Humboldt to the powers of a new invention, photography, which another savant, François Arago, eventually got the French Parliament to adopt.[14] And in 1844, William Henry Fox Talbot published the first book of photographic reproductions under the eloquent title, *The Pencil of Nature.* Among the images he selected, we find a bust of Patroclus rubbing shoulders with a broom leaning against the frame of an open grange door. Spirit had pushed nature out of art, but only at the price of having to take over its legacy by introducing into its productions the very indistinction that nature had embodied in the century of gardens and of the landscape: the indistinction between what is art, and what is not.

Notes

Foreword

1. Cf. *Aisthesis: Scenes from the Aesthetic Regime of Art*, trans. Zakir Paul (London and New York: Verso, 2013), and *Modern Times: Temporality in Art and Politics*, trans. Gregory Elliot (New York: Verso, 2022).

I. A Newcomer to the Fine Arts

1. Kant (1790), p. 151, Ak 5:323 (translation slightly modified).
2. An edited version exists in English: *Theory of Garden Art*, ed. and trans. Linda B. Parshall (Philadelphia: University of Pennsylvania Press, 2001). – Trans.
3. An English translation appeared the same year, entitled *The Garden, Or, The Art of Laying Out Grounds*; another translation appeared in 1805 under the title: *The Gardens: A Poem*. – Trans.
4. Whately (1770), p. 1. Although faithful, Whately's French translator omits the mention "in England,"

93

no doubt in order to avoid ruffling the feathers of his French readers.

5. The *Hypnerotomachia Poliphili*, attributed to Francesco Colonna, was first published in Venice in 1499. – Trans.

6. A. J. Dezallier d'Argenville, *The Theory and Practice of Gardening*, trans. John James (London: B. Lintot, 1712).

7. Guido Giubbini, *Il giardino degli equivoci* (Rome: DeriveApprodi, 2016), pp. 44–45.

8. Charles Batteux, *The Fine Arts Reduced to the Same Principle*, trans. James O. Young (Oxford: Oxford University Press, 2015 [1746]), p. 6.

9. Kant (1790), p. 150, Ak 5:322. (I have changed Meredith's "sensuous" [truth/appearance] to "sensible," in accordance not only with more recent translations of Kant, like Pluhar's or Guyer-Matthews', but also with the standard translation of "*sensible*" in Rancière. – Trans.)

10. Kant (1790), p. 151, Ak 5:323.

11. Ibid., p. 151, footnote no. 16, Ak 5:323.

12. Ibid., p. 154, Ak 5:326.

13. Ibid., pp. 91 and 99, Ak 5:261 and 269.

14. The *Peri Hypsous* is of course the work known in English as *On the Sublime*; although for a long time attributed to Longinus, his authorship of it is doubtful. – Trans.

II. Scenes of Nature

1. Whately (1770), p. 1.

2. La Fontaine, *Fragments du Songe de Vaux* (1671), in *Poèmes et Poésies diverses* (Paris: Garnier, 1924), p. 87.

3. Abbé Dubos, *Critical Reflections on Poetry, Painting and Music, with an Inquiry into the Rise and Progress of the Theatrical Entertainment of the Ancients*, trans. Thomas Nugent (London: John Nourse, 1748 [1719]), vol. 1, pp. 37–42, pp. 56–61.

4. Jean-François de Saint-Lambert, *Les Saisons* (Paris: P. Didot, 1795), p. xvi.

5. Thomas Whately, *L'Art de former les jardins modernes*, trans. François de Paul Latapie (Paris: L. Cellot, 1771), p. 2.

6. Whately (1770), p. 1.

7. Alexander van Humboldt, *Cosmos: Sketch of a Physical Description of the Universe*, ed. Edward Sabine (London: Longman, Brown, Green and Longmans, 1846), p. 3.

8. Alexander Pope, "Epistle IV: To Richard Boyle, Earl of Burlington," in *The Rape of the Lock and other Major Writings*, ed. Leo Damrosch (London: Penguin Books, 2011), p. 167, ll. 117–120.

9. Lord Shaftesbury, *Characteristicks of Men, Manners, Opinions, Times* (Indianapolis: Liberty Fund, 2001 [1737–1738]), p. 220 [394].

10. See Joseph Addison, *Spectator* no. 414 (June 25, 1712).

11. William Hogarth, *The Analysis of Beauty*, ed. Ronald Paulson (New Haven and London: Yale University Press, 1997 [1753]), p. 33.

12. Burke (1757), p. 105.

13. A. Dodsley, "A Description of the Leasowes," in *The Poetical Works of William Shenstone, with the Life of the Author, and a Description of the Leasowes* (London: C. Cooke, 1800 [1765]), p. xix.

14. "Improver" is the name that came to be given to Brown ("capability for improvement") and to the landscape gardeners who emulated his style. – Trans.
15. Price (1794), p. 192.
16. Knight (1794), p. 11, ll. 169–172.
17. Gilpin (1772), vol. 1, p. 194.
18. Ibid., vol. 1, pp. 218–219.
19. Richard Payne Knight, *An Analytical Inquiry into the Principles of Taste* (London: Luke Honsard, 1805), pp. 77–79.
20. Price (1810), vol. 2, pp. 239–240.
21. Ibid., vol. 2, p. 78.
22. Ibid., vol. 2, pp. 79–80.
23. Ibid., pp. 20–21.
24. Knight (1794), p. 10, ll. 143–144.
25. Some of the "essays on painting" can be found in *Diderot's Thoughts on Art and Style, with Some of His Shorter Essays*, ed. and trans. Beatrix L. Tollemache (London and Sydney: Remington & Co., 1893). For the "harmony of movements," see p. 39. – Trans.

III. The Landscape as Painting

1. Price (1794), p. 121.
2. "How many things do the painters see in light and shadow that we do not." The passage is from Cicero's *On Academic Skepticism*. – Trans.
3. Price (1794), p. 5.
4. Price (1810), vol. 2, p. 78.
5. Price (1794), p. 9, unnumbered footnote.
6. Price (1810), vol. 2, p. xiv.
7. Price (1794), p. 14.
8. Knight (1794), p. 6, l. 78.

9. William Marshall, *A Review of The Landscape, A Didactic Poem: Also of An Essay on the Picturesque* (London: G. Nichol, 1795), p. 11.
10. Ibid., p. 45.
11. Ibid., p. 259.
12. Kant (1790), p. 152, Ak 5:323.
13. Whately (1770), p. 118.
14. Ibid., p. 124.
15. Ibid., p. 121.
16. Ibid., p. 122.
17. Horace Walpole, *Essay on Modern Gardening* (Strawberry-Hill: T. Kirgate, 1785), p. 57.
18. Gilpin (1772), vol. 2, p. 11.
19. Ibid., vol. 2, p. 11.
20. Ibid., vol. 2, p. 14.
21. Ibid., vol. 2, p. 15. Gilpin's is paraphrasing a passage in Part 2, Section 9 of Burke's *A Philosophical Enquiry*. See Burke (1757), p. 70.

IV. Beyond the Visible

1. Price (1794), p. 18.
2. See Whately (1770), p. 66.
3. Ibid., pp. 68–69.
4. Ibid., p. 218ff.
5. Ibid., p. 187.
6. Burke (1757), pp. 102ff.
7. Ibid., p. 105.
8. Ibid., p. 68.
9. Ibid., p. 70.
10. Gilpin (1772), vol. 2, p. 11.
11. De Luc (1778), p. 190. (Christian Cay Lorenz Hirschfeld cites this passage in *Theory of Garden Art*, pp. 178–179. – Trans.)

12. Thomas Herring, *Letters to William Duncombe, 1728–1757*, cited in Malcolm Andrews, *The Search for the Picturesque: Landscape Aesthetic and Tourism in Britain, 1760–1800* (Aldershot: Scolar Press, 1989), p. 110.

13. Gilpin (1772), vol. 1, pp. 132–133.

14. Ibid., vol. 1, p. 134.

15. Ibid., vol. 1, pp. 134–135.

16. Ibid., vol. 1, p. 132.

17. Ibid., vol. 1, p. 179.

18. Gilpin (1776), vol. 1, p. 121.

19. Patrick Brydone, *A Tour Through Sicily and Malta: In a Series of Letters to William Beckford* (London: M. Straham and T. Cadell, 1780 [1775]), vol. 1, p. 133. (Cited in Hirschfeld, *Theory of Garden Art*, pp. 182–183. – Trans.)

20. De Luc (1778), p. 106.

21. Jean-Jacques Rousseau, *Julie, or The New Heloise*, trans. and annotated by Philip Stewart and Jean Vaché (Hanover, NH: Dartmouth College Press, 1997), p. 64.

22. Hirschfeld, *Theory of Garden Art*, p. 152.

23. Kant (1790), p. 107, Ak 5:277.

24. Ibid., p. 86, Ak 5:256.

V. Politics of the Landscape

1. William Wordsworth, *The Prelude; or, Growth of a Poet's Mind*, Book VI, ll. 357ff. I discuss Wordsworth's voyage into revolutionary France in *Short Voyages to the Land of the People*, trans. James B. Swenson (Stanford, CA: Stanford University Press, 2003), pp. 9–24.

2. Burke (1790), p. 146.

3. Ibid., p. 65.
4. Ibid., p. 66.
5. Ibid., p. 65.
6. Gilpin (1776), vol. 2, p. 230.
7. See W. G. Hoskins, *The Making of the English Landscape* (London: Hodder and Stoughton Ltd., 1955), pp. 142ff.
8. Tom Williamson and Liz Bellamy, *Property and Landscape: A Social History of Land Ownership and the English Countryside* (London: George Philips, 1987), pp. 137–138.
9. J. M. Neeson, *Commoners: Common Right, Enclosure and Social Change in England, 1700–1820* (Cambridge: Cambridge University Press, 1993), pp. 191–195.
10. Humphry Repton, Letter to Uvedale Price (July 1, 1794), reprinted in Price (1810), vol. 3, p. 10.
11. "O Harmony, once more from heav'n descend! / Mould the stiff lines, and the harsh colours blend; / Banish the formal fir's unsocial shade, / And crop th'aspiring larche's saucy head." Knight (1794), p. 54, ll. 57–60.
12. Edmund Burke, Letter to the Duke of Richmond (November 17, 1774), in *Selected Letters of Edmund Burke*, ed. Harvey C. Mansfield (Chicago: The University of Chicago Press, 1984), p. 184.
13. De Luc (1778), p. 134.
14. Knight (1794), p. 73, ll. 415–416, and p. 71, ll. 387ff (respectively).
15. Price (1810), vol. 2, p. 344, unnumbered footnote.
16. Price (1794), pp. 278–279.
17. Price (1810), vol. 3, pp. 178–179.
18. Knight (1794), p. 73, ll. 419–420.

19. Uvedale Price, cited in Daniels, "The Political Iconography of Woodland in Later Georgian England," in *The Iconography of Landscape: Essays on the Symbolic Representation, Design and Use of Past Environments*, eds. Denis Cosgrove and Stephen Daniels (Cambridge: Cambridge University Press, 1988), p. 63.
20. Kant (1790), p. 152, Ak 5:323.

Epilogue
1. Hegel (1835), vol. 1, p. 131.
2. The lectures were not published, but they supplied the material that Humboldt would later publish in *Cosmos* (1845), where the aesthetic anticipation of the scientific connection among natural phenomena is constantly affirmed and illustrated.
3. Gustav Carus, *Nine Letters on Landscape Painting: Written in the Years 1815–1824, with a Letter from Goethe by Way of Introduction*, trans. David Britt (Los Angeles: Getty Research Institute, 2002), pp. 118–119. See also Roland Recht, *La Lettre de Humboldt: Du jardin paysager au daguerréotype* (Paris: C. Bourgois, 1989), and Élisabeth Décultot, *Peindre le paysage: discours théorique et renouveau pictural dans le romantisme allemand* (Tusson: Du Lérot, 1996).
4. Hegel (1835), vol. 1, pp. 131–132.
5. Ibid., vol. 1, p. 31.
6. Ibid., vol. 1, p. 162.
7. "Toward the vault of the Eternal Heaven my eye does rise / toward You, Oh Brilliant Star of the Night; / and the forgetting of all wishes, all hopes, / streams down upon me from Your Eternity. / Sense

is lost in contemplation, what I called mine does vanish, / unto the Boundless do I myself abandon. / I am in it, am everything, am only it." G. W. F. Hegel, "Eleusis" (1796), in *Hegel, the Letters*, trans. Clark Butler and Christiane Seiler (Bloomington: Indiana University Press, 1984), p. 46.

8. Friedrich Hölderlin, *The Death of Empedocles: A Mourning-Play*, trans. David Farrell Krell (Albany: State University of New York, 2008), p. 90, ll. 1505ff.

9. F. W. J. Schelling, Letter to Hegel (July 11, 1803), cited in *Hegel, the Letters*, p. 66.

10. Hegel (1835), vol. 2, p. 700.

11. Ibid., vol. 2, p. 700.

12. Ibid., vol. 1, pp. 43–44.

13. Cf. Ingrid Oesterle, "Récit d'un voyage à Paris: métropole et paysage chez Carl Gustav Carus (1835)," in *Revue germanique internationale* no. 7 (1997): 137–138.

14. Cf. Recht, *Lettre de Humboldt*.